50
50
Monologues for
Student Actors
II

DEPNER

m̄p™

MERIWETHER PUBLISHING LTD.
Colorado Springs, Colorado

Meriwether Publishing Ltd., Publisher
PO Box 7710
Colorado Springs, CO 80933-7710

www.meriwether.com

Editor: Theodore O. Zapel
Assistant editor: Nicole Rutledge
Cover design: Jan Melvin

Library of Congress Cataloging-in-Publication Data

Depner, Mary.
    50/50 monologues for student actors II : 100 more monologues for guys and girls / by Mary Depner. -- 1st ed.
        p. cm.
    ISBN 978-1-56608-188-7
    1. Monologues. 2. Acting--Auditions. I. Title. II. Title: Fifty/fifty monologues for student actors II.
    PN2080.D466 2012
    808.82'45--dc23

                                    2012029295

1   2   3   12   13   14

This book is dedicated to
my favorite poet in the universe,
my mom, S. L. Depner
(a.k.a. Sally, Fred, and sometimes José).

Table of Contents

About the Author

Monologues
for Girls

1. Frozen

1   I've been frozen for the past three years. Ever since my
2 daddy died, it's like I've been living in a dream. I go about
3 my business. I go to school. I do my work. But something
4 changed in me three years ago and I can't seem to change
5 it back. I guess it was survival mode that brought about the
6 change. My emotions were put on hold. All of my hopes and
7 dreams for my family and me ... put away. Forever. Nothing
8 I wanted to do for my daddy could ever be done now. I know
9 people do things in someone's memory, but I really don't
10 buy into that. You have to do for someone when they are
11 alive. You have to do for the living. I do want to live my life
12 in a way that would have made him proud. I think I owe him
13 that. But I don't believe he'll know it. I wish I did believe it.
14 I really do. I envy people with that belief. They say things
15 like, "I know Johnny's looking down today and smiling." You
16 know, stuff like that. It's sweet. It really is. But for me, I
17 believe that my daddy has moved on. Any chance I might
18 have had to show him my appreciation is gone. Vanished. I
19 think what it would take for me to "thaw out," so to speak,
20 to be fully myself again, would be to find someone who loves
21 me as much as my daddy did. And someone I could likewise
22 love in return. I know you think I'm too young to feel that
23 way. I know I'm supposed to be thinking about where I'd like
24 to go to college, or who's gonna ask me to the prom. I know.
25 But that's not what I think about at all. I used to be like
26 that, but I'm the sadder and wiser me now. I just wish I
27 wouldn't have turned to ice. It's gonna make it so much
28 harder to find someone to love me now. I'm not the bubbly,

1 happy-go-lucky girl I once was. I can only hope that someone
2 will find that appealing and try to break the ice. *(Pause)* **And**
3 if not, I think I'll try to spend some time just sitting in the
4 sun each day, trying to reflect on the beauty that still lives
5 in the world. It warms me and seems like it will help.
6 Eventually.

2. The Perfect Date

1   It was the perfect date. *(Sighs.)* Well, first of all for those
2 of you who don't know me, let me give you some
3 background. I have had a crush on John Jamieson since we
4 were in Mrs. Holmes' class in the first grade. I know it
5 sounds ridiculous, but it's true. I can still remember stealing
6 a glimpse of him every time I got the chance. And while Mrs.
7 Holmes was pontificating about the alphabet or some such
8 thing at the blackboard, I was off and running.
9 Daydreaming, that is. Yep, you guessed it. I was dreaming
10 of John and me. We would be walking hand in hand across
11 the playground. Or sitting next to each other in the cafeteria
12 sharing secrets and giggles over lunch. Of course, I never
13 actually told John that I liked him. Noooo. I was much too
14 shy for that. It was, you know, always just a fantasy. So
15 anyway, you can imagine how this date the other night with
16 John felt for me. It was amazing. Well, first of all he picked
17 me up in his cute little red convertible. All the girls in the
18 neighborhood were sitting on Patty Simon's porch across
19 the street and you should have seen the look on their faces.
20 I think Patty's jaw dropped down to her knees. John got out
21 of the car and he looked soooo hot. I didn't look so bad
22 either, if I must say so myself. I had on my favorite black
23 leather mini skirt and well ... John really couldn't take his
24 eyes off me. We got in the car and he sped me away into the
25 twilight. We went to Tabitha's for a romantic candlelit dinner
26 out on the wharf. Then afterwards, we went for a really long
27 walk on the beach. It was such a beautiful night. We talked
28 and talked as we walked hand in hand under the stars. Oh,

1   yes. He kissed me. *(Sighs.)* **We walked all the way to the**
2   **jetties and before we knew it the sun was coming up and we**
3   **were watching the breaking dawn.** *(Sits thinking it over silently*
4   *for a minute.)* **Hmmmm? What happened next? Oh, I woke**
5   **up, of course. No, not at the beach, at home in my bed. Oh,**
6   **you didn't think I really had a date with John did you?**
7   *(Laughs.)* **Oh, no silly, it was just a dream. John and I never**
8   **even talk at school and he doesn't have a clue that I'm mad**
9   **about him. Tell him? Oh, no, I could never do that. He'll**
10 **always be my fantasy, but that's OK. I'll cherish our perfect**
11 **date forever.**

3. Faith, Hope, and Charity

1   My mother always goes around the house singing this
2   song about faith, hope, and charity. And she always says
3   that charity is the most important of all. I think she may be
4   right, but sometimes I wish she would think like some
5   people do, that charity should begin at home. I mean, every
6   weekend my mom is busy working on some charity event.
7   She can't pass up a good cause. But sometimes I feel
8   neglected. It's like, I need her time too, you know. And she's
9   always asking me if I really need something that I haven't
10   used in a while or if I'd like to donate it to a good cause. I've
11   started hiding my stuff instead of trying to persuade her
12   that even though I haven't used it for a year, I might really
13   want it some day. *(Sighs.)* I mean, it is nice that everyone
14   tells me what a great mother I have all the time. So many
15   people tell me she's meant so much to them and helped
16   them get through some really rough times. But what about
17   me? What about my tough times? Does she ever have time
18   to worry about that? If I try to tell her about something that
19   happened to me at school that made me cry, or something
20   I wanted, like to be president of student council, that I didn't
21   get, she just frowns at me and says something like,
22   "Remember there are those soooo much less fortunate than
23   you. I'm not sure I can feel sorry for you when there are
24   children who will go to bed tonight with nothing to eat."
25   Sometimes I wonder if I will ever get her sympathy or
26   attention for anything. A few months ago was the real
27   topper. She brought home a "little sister" and said she'd be
28   spending time with this girl who needed a positive influence

1   in her life. She was going to take her to a carnival that had
2   just come to town and then do a little shopping. She looked
3   at me, almost like an afterthought, and said, "You don't
4   want to come along, do you?" I was like, "Yeah, I do! I like
5   carnivals and shopping, too!" I swear, I think my mother
6   was almost disappointed that I came along. But I could be
7   wrong. It did turn out to be a really nice day. And my mom's
8   little sister had a really great time. At the end of the day she
9   said something that made me get tears in my eyes. She
10 said, "This was such a wonderful day! I wish I could put it
11 in my heart and keep it forever." She was really sweet. It
12 made me have faith that good deeds do make a difference.
13 And it gave me hope that by helping others we can make the
14 world a better place. I went to bed feeling so proud of my
15 mother. I wondered if my mother knew that there were two
16 girls who really needed her that day.

4. The Bully Busters

1   My friends and I are not the kind to sit back and watch
2 as injustices take place. We don't think kids are helpless.
3 And we believe that actions speak louder than words. That's
4 why we started a group called "The Bully Busters" this year
5 at school. We're a support group for any kids who feel like
6 they're the victims of bullying. It's really cool because we
7 found a great sponsor, Mrs. Cavendish. We have an advisory
8 board made up of parents, teachers, administrators, and
9 counseling professionals from our community who are there
10 for guidance and support. I'm not sure if we'll be successful
11 in our small fight against the wrongdoers, the bullies, the
12 people who I like to say "must have nothing better to do."
13 But at least we're trying. And I think it is really true that
14 there is strength in numbers. And we have a pretty large
15 group. We started out small with only four kids, but now
16 we've got seventy-five members. And some of our members
17 are the coolest kids in school! I hope we can be there for
18 kids when they really need us. I mean, if we can help just
19 one kid in a school of one thousand then, to me, we'll have
20 been a success. And every one of our members will be a real
21 and true superhero. Better than any comic strip hero ever
22 could be.

5. Total Sister Eclipse

1   In my family there are three girls. No boys. Yep, there's
2 just me, my big sister Amy, and my little sister Sam. Oh,
3 and my parents, of course. Wouldn't want to leave them out,
4 would I? Well, I mean, sometimes I would. But anyway, you
5 see, the point I'd like to make is that sometimes it seems
6 like they don't notice me at all. I mean my parents and my
7 sisters. But especially my parents. Well, that's because of
8 my sisters, of course. You see, my sisters, Amy and Sam,
9 are not ordinary girls. They are both "exceedingly gifted."
10 Well, they're exceedingly gifted in very different ways, but
11 the point is they both far outshine me. Me? I'm average. Yes,
12 just average. Well, when I say that my sisters are gifted I
13 mean really, really gifted. So maybe I wouldn't seem average
14 in a normal family, but in my family I'm extremely, extremely
15 average. Or maybe even below average, I suppose. Sam, my
16 little sister, is a genius. Seriously. I'm not exaggerating.
17 Well, for instance, the local newspaper interviewed her when
18 she was three. During the interview Sam recited one of
19 Shakespeare's sonnets. I am still not really sure what a
20 sonnet is. No, no, please don't tell me. I really, really don't
21 want to know. My sister Amy? She's beautiful. Yes, yes, I
22 know that a lot of girls are beautiful. But Amy? She is
23 "stunningly," "breathtakingly" beautiful. Everyone says so. I
24 mean, truly. I don't think a day has gone by that I can
25 remember when somebody hasn't said so. Me? I'm OK.
26 Really? Thanks. But seriously, I'm not fishing for
27 compliments. And I'm not looking for sympathy. Well, OK,
28 maybe just a little sympathy. And why shouldn't I? Who

1 wouldn't? I mean, really. Do you have any idea what it's like
2 to be me? Nothing I ever do measures up. Or ever will. It's
3 like my sisters are so brilliant, so bright, so beautiful, that
4 no one can see past them to see me. I guess you could say
5 it's a total eclipse. Right? A total sister eclipse. Don't you
6 see? Hey, are you listening to me? *(Turns around.)* Oh. Hi,
7 Amy, I didn't hear you come in. *(Looks back at friend and*
8 *murmurs.)* OK! Well, enough about me, then. Right? I'll just,
9 um, disappear.

6. A Will of Her Own

1   There are no two ways about it. My sister, Bethany
2 Louise Bartel, is weird. No, not just weird. Incredibly,
3 undeniably, certifiably weird. Oh, please, your sister
4 Michelle is not weird. Not in comparison to Bethany. Even
5 my parents acknowledge that there is something different
6 about Bethany. I'm not saying that I'm not a little weird too.
7 I just don't let it show as much as Bethany does. It's like
8 my dad always says, "Everybody has a freak flag, OK. Some
9 people just don't fly theirs as much as others." Well, let me
10 tell you, my sister Bethany flies hers at the top of the pole.
11 Give you an example? OK, when Bethany was little and was
12 starting to learn to read she used to pick up my dad's paper
13 after he was done with it. We'd find her sitting in the corner
14 at age six reading the paper. Wait a minute. That's not the
15 weirdest part. The weirdest part is that she wasn't just
16 reading any old part of the paper. She was reading the
17 obituaries. Yeah, the obituaries. Then she would cut out the
18 ones that she liked and put them on a bulletin board on her
19 bedroom wall. Some of them were "so good" she made
20 collages out of them and stuck them on the refrigerator with
21 magnets. They were kind of good. I mean, like if the paper
22 said that somebody who died used to like to go sailing,
23 she'd put their picture in the middle of the page and cut out
24 sailboats from magazine ads and junk like that. It was weird
25 though, right? I mean, she didn't even know these people.
26 Then when she turned seven. I'll never forget this. When she
27 turned seven we had this big party for Bethany and were
28 making movies. Somebody took the camera and they asked

1 her all about how it felt to be seven years old. Then
2 somebody says, "So, Bethany, what do you want to be when
3 you grow up?" And she looks up and says, without blinking
4 an eye, "A Wills and Probate lawyer". I think the whole room
5 got silent. I was like, "How did you come up with that?" I
6 mean, I could see if one of our relatives was a lawyer or
7 something like that, but my family is totally in the pastry
8 business, you know. Of course you know, who doesn't,
9 right? So anyway, here's this room full of bakers going,
10 "What did she just say?" But my dad's just like, "Cool!" So
11 I don't get it, but Bethany, she's just totally marching to her
12 own drum as my Aunt Shirley says. The other day I went in
13 her room to see if she had any of our old board games. She
14 was playing pretend and I thought she was playing school.
15 You know, like we used to do. But she wasn't. She was
16 pretending to be a lawyer. She was talking to these
17 imaginary "clients" and helping them to decide what would
18 happen to all their money and their belongings when they,
19 you know, kicked the bucket. I was like, "Bethany, what is
20 it with you and this obsession?" She just shrugged. I looked
21 at the paper she was writing on and it looked like her
22 "clients" were pretty darn rich. They had a Rolls Royce, a
23 yacht, and six Burmese tigers. I was like, "Bethany, don't
24 you want to go outside and play? Or maybe you could help
25 me wash my car. I'll give you five bucks." Bethany thought
26 about it for a second and then she said, "I would, but my
27 clients have been waiting for weeks to see me and my next
28 available appointment won't be for another three months."
29 That's Bethany. She's weird. Or as my mother would say,
30 "She has a will of her own."

7. From Here I Dream

1   This is my bedroom. Do you like it? Thanks. Oh, you like
2   the red wall? I painted that wall red last year during Spring
3   Break. It took quite a bit of persuading for my mother to let
4   me do it, but I guess it turned out really well. Yeah.
5   Hmmmm? Oh, those? That's a little collection of dollhouse
6   miniatures that my grandmother gave me. Just before she
7   died. She collected them. She actually had a huge collection
8   of miniatures and she divided them among the grandkids.
9   There's seven of us, so ... I got these. This one is my
10   favorite. See, it's a little miniature sewing machine. My
11   grandmother was a really good seamstress. She made
12   things for all of the grandkids. She made that quilt on my
13   bed. *(Sees her friend noticing a photograph.)* That's a picture
14   of my dad in high school. Funny, isn't it? He looks a little bit
15   like Hughie McGregor, doesn't he? *(Laughs.)* Looks nothing
16   at all like him now, though. No, he doesn't live here. He lives
17   in Kentucky. Uh huh, my parents got divorced when I was
18   five. We're still close though, my dad and I. We talk on the
19   phone almost every day. And I spend summers there. In
20   Kentucky. Want to know what my favorite thing about my
21   room is? *(Opening the curtain and the sliding glass door)* My
22   favorite thing about this room is the balcony. It's a beautiful
23   view, isn't it? Come on out and have a seat. Isn't it
24   gorgeous? I love the mountains. I can sit out here for hours.
25   I just sit here and think and dream. What do I dream about?
26   Oh, a lot of things. A lot of things. I dream about all the
27   things I want to accomplish. I dream about adventures I'd
28   like to have. I'd like to see Paris one day. The Eiffel Tower,

1 you know. I dream about being a famous author. Well, yeah,
2 I write a little. But I'd like to write more. To write a novel.
3 Just something wonderful that is adored by the masses. A
4 *New York Times* Best Seller. You know, just a little dream.
5 *(Smiles and then gets serious.)* Sometimes, lately, when I'm
6 out here, I dream about you. *(Looks down.)* I hope I'm not
7 embarrassing you. I know I'm embarrassing myself. It's just
8 that ever since we met, I knew ... I mean, there was
9 something about you. So yeah, I've been dreaming a little
10 about you and me. And only you can tell me ... is there a
11 possibility that my dreams might come true? *(Listening, then*
12 *puts her head down and smiles a little.)* That's good to know.

8. So This Is Love

1   I haven't eaten anything all day. I'm glad my mother
2 hasn't noticed. She's all excited about the new house she's
3 showing. I just feel so ... out of it. Like I'm in a daze. And
4 it all happened so quickly. So unexpectedly, too. I totally
5 went to Meredith's party expecting to be bored. I mean,
6 Meredith and I are only really "friends" because of our
7 mothers. I mean, they hang out together all the time. So I
8 just went to be nice. I'm just usually not too into the crowd
9 that Meredith hangs out with. So there I was at this party,
10 which was pretty lame, when suddenly I noticed this guy in
11 the corner was staring at me. And he was actually really
12 cute. All of a sudden he gets up and walks over to me and
13 asks me if I'd like to dance. The music had been blasting for
14 about an hour, but nobody was dancing. I was like, "Sure,
15 why not?" We danced and then we went out on Meredith's
16 patio and sat on her hammock and talked for about an hour.
17 He was so sweet. And funny, too. And well, the rest as they
18 say is history. *(Sighs.)* He took my phone number but he
19 hasn't called yet. Do you think he will? Oh my gosh. I'm just
20 in such a daze. This must be love, right? I've never felt this
21 way before. It's like butterflies in my stomach and just this
22 totally surreal feeling. It's so amazing. Me, in love? It just
23 hit me out of the blue. I hope he calls. Do you think he will?
24 Oh my gosh, my phone is ringing. It's him, it's him! *(Holds*
25 *the phone to her heart and closes her eyes for a minute.)* **So this**
26 **is love.** *(Pause)* **Hello, this is Mandy.**

9. Jealous?

1   I am not jealous and I have nothing against Allison
2 Fannigan. I just think it's unfair. What is unfair? Are you
3 kidding? Do you know Allison Fannigan? OK, well, then you
4 obviously know that Allison Fannigan is probably the
5 luckiest girl in the world. Well, OK, she is at least the
6 luckiest girl at Harrison High. And what's not fair is that
7 there is probably only so much good luck to go around
8 within a certain, let's say fifty-mile radius, and Allison
9 Fannigan is obviously sucking it all up and not leaving any
10 good luck for the rest of us. And that is particularly me. Oh,
11 puleeze. Am I not the most obviously unlucky girl in the
12 universe? OK, well, at least the most unlucky girl at
13 Harrison High. Well, there you go. At least we agree on
14 something. Don't you see the obvious correlation? Allison is
15 super lucky. I'm super unlucky. Obviously, if Allison weren't
16 such a good-luck hog, I might have a little good luck for
17 myself. Don't laugh, it's true. OK, so you don't believe me,
18 but it's true. I am not being jealous. I'm not. Geez, you
19 sound like my mother. She's always saying, *(Mimicking her*
20 *voice)* "Jealousy doesn't look good on you, dear." No, this is
21 not about being jealous, this is totally about the science of
22 fortune, good and bad. Seriously. I am totally looking at this
23 from a scientific viewpoint. In fact, I might do a science
24 project on this for next year's science fair. I could create
25 some really convincing posters. I mean, on paper, it would
26 all be so clear. Take Allison. Well, let's say she's probably
27 had fifty dates this year. *Moi?* Roughly zero. On my birthday
28 this year, it was announced that Allison was voted president

1   of the sophomore class. Yours truly? Got a detention that
2   day for being late three times to Algebra and a traffic ticket
3   for speeding in an attempt not to be late three times for
4   Algebra. Last summer vacation Allison and her family went
5   to London. Me? Had chicken pox and caused my whole
6   family to miss out on our annual trip to Disney World. I
7   won't bore you with all the other details, but as you can see,
8   I have a solid case. The evidence will prove, Allison
9   Fannigan is a good luck vacuum at Harrison High and
10 something, my friend, has got to be done about it. Jealousy
11 has nothing to do with it. It's about justice, not jealousy.
12 But I'm not gonna stand here and defend myself 'til I'm blue
13 in the face. I'm gonna prove it. You'll see. And when I do, I'll
14 win first prize at the science fair. And then somebody's
15 gonna be jealous and it won't be me.

10. Priceless

1   It was the summer after seventh grade and Jessie and I
2 were hanging out at the mall. We had been inseparable since
3 we met that year during the spring play. We both got lousy
4 parts in it, of course, so we had a lot of time to goof around
5 during rehearsals. Jessie thought I was hilarious. I thought
6 Jessie had everything I'd always wanted and more. She was
7 smart and pretty. All the boys thought she was cool. I guess
8 you could say that Jessie was everything I wasn't. So
9 anyway, like I said, it was summer and we were hanging out
10 at the mall. Jessie had money to buy a new bathing suit so
11 we'd been looking for a red bikini. That's what Jessie
12 wanted, anyway. We went into this surf shop for teens and
13 Jessie started trying stuff on. I walked over to the counter
14 to try on sunglasses and saw this box that said, "Win a
15 thousand-dollar shopping spree." I asked the clerk how you
16 won and she said you had to write a short paragraph,
17 twenty-five words or less, on what the beach meant to you.
18 I asked her for two entry forms and stuck them in my purse.
19 Jessie came out of the dressing room in a really cute red
20 bikini. I said, "Do you think your mom will let you wear it?"
21 She said, "Yeah. My mom lets me do anything." So, Jessie
22 bought the suit and we went to the food court for pizza. I
23 took out the entry forms, gave Jessie hers, and started
24 writing my paragraph. Jessie smiled and said, "I've got a
25 cool idea. Why don't you put my name on yours and I'll put
26 your name on mine. You know, switch identities." I was like,
27 "OK, but mine is gonna win." Jessie said, "Really? We'll
28 see." So we wrote our paragraphs. I put Jessie's name and

1 number on my form and she put mine on hers. About two
2 months later, my mom and I were at the mall. We were
3 passing the surf shop and when I looked in the window I
4 almost fell over. There on this poster was this big picture of
5 Jessie with my words, my paragraph, in big, bold letters
6 under her face. I looked through the window and there she
7 was with her mom. She was loading up on clothes, bathing
8 suits, and flip flops that should have been mine. I walked in
9 the store and said, "What are you doing? Didn't you tell
10 them it was me?" Jessie acted like she didn't have a clue
11 what I was talking about. And pretty much like she had
12 never seen me before in her life. Her mother said, "Young
13 lady, it's not nice to be a sore loser. Maybe you'll get it next
14 time." My mom came into the store a few minutes later and
15 asked me what was wrong. I could barely talk. "Nothing," I
16 said. I never spoke to Jessie again after that day, but I did
17 slide a note in her locker on the first day of school. It may
18 not have been as good as my contest winning paragraph,
19 but it was definitely short and to the point. I just wrote, "A
20 bunch of junk from the surf shop — a thousand bucks.
21 Finding out the truth about someone you thought was your
22 friend — Priceless."

11. Kids, Don't Try This at Home

1   I hate you, Mom! No. I won't take it back. I will not. I
2 meant it. I mean it. I do!
3   My life is horrible and it's your fault. We used to be a
4 family. We used to have meals together and take trips
5 together and live in a house for crying out loud. Now we're
6 stuck in this lousy apartment and I never see Dad because
7 you chased him away. Yes, you did! You did. You chased him
8 away with your constant complaining and whining and
9 screaming. I was there. I ought to know. Good reason? You
10 had a good reason? Good enough to ruin my life? You
11 weren't happy. You weren't happy? Well, what about me,
12 Mom? Did you ever, ever, once stop to think about me? Your
13 daughter? Remember me? You don't love me. Don't lie.
14 *(Screams.)* **I said stop lying!** *(Crying, throws herself on the bed.)*
15 **Get out! Please! Get out of my room.** *(Through her tears)* **You**
16 **love me about as much as you loved Dad. Which is** *not at*
17 *all. (Through her tears)* **You're lying again** *(Sobbing)* **You never,**
18 **ever loved Dad. I heard you. I said, "I heard you!" I heard**
19 you that day when you were on the phone with Aunt Lilly. I
20 heard you distinctly say that you never, ever loved Dad. I
21 heard you say that you married him for security and then
22 you said, "And what a joke that turned out to be." I was not
23 eavesdropping. I was walking into the living room in my own
24 house. Our house. Our family's house. You thought Dad and
25 I had gone to the store, but he brought me back so that I
26 could run in and get my phone. And that's when I heard you
27 and found out the truth. All your bickering at Dad and all
28 your lies to me about how you and Dad used to love each

1   other but things had changed. *(Shaking her head)* **Mom.**

2   **Why? Why? I used to love you so much. Why? Why? Why did**

3   **you have to make me hate you like this?**

12. Blah

1   Blah, blah, blah, blah, blah. I might as well be speaking
2   gibberish. Nobody listens to me anyway. I'm serious. Are
3   you even listening to me right now? Are you sure? I could
4   have sworn for a minute that I saw that faraway look in your
5   eye. You know, the one my mother gets, my sister gets, my
6   father gets, my teachers get, the minute I open my mouth
7   and start to speak. I'm so used to it, you know, nobody
8   listening to me. So I guess I feel sort of like I can say
9   anything and it won't matter. I guess that's what's
10   happened to me, anyway. Yesterday. Yesterday, I wish I
11   hadn't said anything at all. Yesterday in drama class we had
12   to go to the dance room for the whole period because our
13   classroom didn't have any air conditioning. So we went to
14   the dance room just to kind of hang out for fourth period.
15   Mrs. Violet, our drama teacher, tried to keep us all in line,
16   but the kids were acting sort of crazy. There's this whole
17   wall that's a mirror and everybody got all goofy making
18   faces and dancing around. They were basically acting like
19   jerks. Mrs. Violet was losing it. She looked so frustrated
20   and exhausted from it all. I don't know why I said it, but I
21   said, "Why are your wasting your life teaching middle
22   school, anyway?" She looked at me for a second, but she
23   didn't answer. I didn't think twice about it, 'cause like I said,
24   nobody ever listens to me. But, today ... today when I went
25   to drama class Mrs. Violet wasn't there and everybody was
26   talking about it. How she was gone and all. I mean, they say
27   she just quit. Just like that. I'm gonna miss Mrs. Violet.
28   She was a really good teacher. Finally, I guess, somebody
29   listened to me.

13. Getting to Know You

1   *(Coming into the basement)* **What are you doing down**
2   **here? I came down here to get away from Mom and Dad's**
3   **arguing so that I can do my homework. Go back upstairs.**
4   **Yes. You don't need to be down here. You don't have any**
5   **homework and if you did you wouldn't do it anyway. So go**
6   **on, get out.** *(Sighs.)* **Well, I'm down here to work, so if you're**
7   **staying ...** *don't bother me!* **Fine. Fine.** *(Gets settled with her*
8   *books and laptop.)* **It's cold in here.** *(Sighs.)* **I hate math.**
9   **Hmmmm? Oh, I just said, "I hate math." What? Yeah right,**
10   **you love math. I'm sure.** *(Sighs.)* **That's why you practically**
11   **failed basic math two years in a row. Todd, the only reason**
12   **you passed basic math last year was because Mrs.**
13   **Brickman desperately wanted you to pass so that she**
14   **wouldn't have to see your face in her class another year. It**
15   **is true.** *(Laughs.)* **What did you say? A genius? You're a math**
16   **genius? Right. And I'm the Queen of England.** *(Sighs.)*
17   **What's that? You could have taught basic math? OK, Todd,**
18   **enough. I've got work to do. I can't play around. If you're**
19   **going to bother me, please just go upstairs. What? What did**
20   **you just say under your breath? Yes, you did. I heard you.**
21   **You just said that I just like to think that I'm the brain of**
22   **the family. Oh, really? I never said that I was the brain of**
23   **the family. I do get the best grades in the family, though,**
24   **don't I? Yeah. And that is because I work for them. I'm not**
25   **always out having fun with my friends or down here in the**
26   **basement doing whatever it is you're doing which is usually**
27   **a whole lot of nothing. What are you doing, anyway?**
28   **Meditating? Meditating? Great. So meditate more quietly**

1   please. I've got work to do. I started it? I started what? The
2   conversation? A conversation with you? No. I did not. I was
3   sitting here trying to get started on my math assignment
4   and I said one little thing to myself, in a conversation with
5   myself, and you butted in. Yeah, that's right, a conversation
6   with myself. Don't tell me you've never had one. A
7   conversation ... with yourself. Oh, yeah? Well, maybe that's
8   your problem. Maybe you should try it some time. A
9   conversation just between you and you. You could start by
10 asking yourself, *(Mimics goofy, surfer voice)* "Hey, dude, if I'm
11 such a genius, a math genius, why did I get a D in basic
12 math *two years in a row?*" Go ahead. Ask yourself. I didn't
13 hear you? OK, you asked yourself silently. So please share.
14 What did yourself answer silently back? What? Yeah, right.
15 You got a D in math two years in a row so that I could feel
16 like the brain of the family and you know for a fact that
17 you're never going to need an A in math for any reason in
18 life. OK, so let's just pretend for a minute that you did get
19 a D in math so that I could feel special. That would be a
20 really stupid thing to do. And you definitely will need good
21 grades in math to get into college. You're not. You're not
22 going to college? Do Mom and Dad know that? Oh, yes, they
23 will care. They care about you as much as they do me. Oh,
24 yes they do. Don't kid yourself. I just get more attention
25 because I'm the girl. Of course it's not fair. There's nothing
26 I can do about it is there? I can't help it that I'm a girl and
27 you're not. You get other things that I don't. Like more
28 freedom. Yeah, freedom. Did you ever think that it might be
29 very confining to have so much attention placed on me? I
30 can't get away with anything. In fact, right now, I bet Mom
31 and Dad are wondering where I am. I should be in my room
32 as usual, listening to them rant and rave and doing my
33 homework. While in the meantime you're down in the
34 basement. Meditating. *(Sighs.)* It's so unfair. What? Maybe I
35 should try it? Meditating? Yeah, right. I've got fifteen really

1   hard math problems to do by tomorrow morning and then
2   there's English homework after that. I wish I was like you
3   and didn't care. But I do. How did we get such different
4   DNA, you and I? Oh, crap, there's Mom. Yeah! Yeah, Mom,
5   I'm down here in the basement. Doing my homework. *(Looks*
6   *at her brother and shakes her head.)* **Yeah, it is kind of cold**
7   **down here. I'll be up in a minute.** *(Resigned, starts collecting*
8   *her things and is about to climb the stairs.)* **I guess the storm is**
9   **over up there. Yeah, I'll be fine. Yeah, right, I'll let you know**
10 **if I need any help with the math. You let me know if you need**
11 **any counseling on the meditation thing, OK.** *(Smiles.)*

14. Boo Hoo

1   Oh, boo hoo. Poor you. Poor, poor, you. Always feeling
2   sorry for yourself, aren't you? Well, I'm tired of it. I'm sick of
3   it. Yeah, you and your whining and crying and boo-hoo-
4   hooing are making me sick. You think I have it made? You
5   think everything for me is just easy breezy, don't you. Well
6   I've got some news for you. It's not. You know, you're just
7   like this girl Theresa I used to work with at the Bacon and
8   Egg Jamboree before the Health Department closed it down.
9   That girl Theresa never smiled. We were supposed to greet
10 people when they came in the door with a smile and say,
11 *(Smiling)* "Welcome to The Bacon and Egg Jamboree. How
12 many in your party on this beautiful morning?" Well, Theresa
13 just wouldn't smile and finally Mrs. Robertson, our
14 manager, said, "Theresa, I'm gonna sit here in the lobby and
15 watch you. The next time a customer walks in I'd better see
16 you smile." So Mrs. Robertson sits there and waits. It only
17 took a few minutes for somebody to come in the door. It was
18 an elderly couple and Mrs. Robertson gives Theresa the nod,
19 like "*go ahead!*" So Theresa, she walks up to the couple and
20 she's like, *(Frowns.)* "Welcome to the Bacon and Egg
21 Jamboree. How many in your party this beautiful morning?"
22 She might as well have said, "How many in your party this
23 miserable, horrible, rotten day?!" Mrs. Robertson fired
24 Theresa on the spot 'cause she refused to smile. And she
25 had it coming. *(Sighs.)* See, people like you and Theresa
26 probably think that you're real special, right? You think that
27 all the tough breaks have been especially handed out to you.
28 Well, surprise, surprise, you couldn't be more wrong. We all

1   get the works every now and then. But, and here's the
2   difference, most people don't wear their problems on their
3   sleeve, or their face, like Theresa. Most people try to put on
4   a smile for other people, and a brave face, too. It's the
5   mature thing to do. Like take me for instance, there's a lot
6   of stuff that I could tell you about that would make you feel
7   really, really sorry for me. But, I don't. I don't tell you 'cause
8   I'm not looking to make you feel bad for me. I'm not trying
9   to bring you down. I'm not looking for your sympathy. I could
10 easily be pitied, but that's not what I want. No. I do not want
11 to be pitied. But I could tell you some stories alright. Like
12 what? You really want to know? OK, I'll tell you something.
13 You know how every weekend you pass the Plucky Clucky
14 restaurant and see Plucky Clucky himself standing on the
15 side of the road with a sign that says "Eight pieces of
16 Chicken for $14.99?" *(Sighs.)* Well, that's me under that
17 chicken suit. Yes, it's true. I'm Plucky Clucky. Yeah, that's
18 me. So every weekend, when most of the kids our age are
19 out having fun, I'm walking up and down in front of Plucky
20 Clucky's carrying a big, heavy, wooden sign. And that's not
21 all. I get abuse out there. Yeah, people are always yelling,
22 "Get a job!" which is the dumbest thing I've ever heard,
23 since that is my job. Yeah, people are mean. Sometimes
24 they don't just yell. Sometimes they throw things at me.
25 Well, like an egg. Yeah, somebody throws an egg just about
26 once every weekend. Last weekend somebody threw ice.
27 Yep. It hit my hand and cut me. Yeah, ice is hard. See. Look
28 at this. *(Holds out her hand.)* Plucky Clucky needs better
29 gloves obviously. So anyway, I don't need your pity. I already
30 told you that. I just want you to know, that you're not alone.
31 There are a lot of other people out there who aren't having
32 a picnic every day. I mean, it is nice to have someone to talk
33 about it with, but, geez Louise, I just think, well, *(Looks*
34 *rather sad.)* I just think it's got to get better, you know.

15. I Don't Want to Go to School

1   *(At the breakfast table)* **I don't want to go to school today.**
2   **What do you mean I never want to go to school? That's not**
3   **true. No, I'm just, I'm so tired of it. I'm not behind in any**
4   **of my classes. One day off would not be a big deal.** *(Pauses.)*
5   **Please pass the syrup.** *(Pours the syrup on and takes a big bite*
6   *of pancake. Chewing)* **I mean, school is like the biggest waste**
7   **of time.** *(Taking another bite)* **Please pass the bacon.** *(Puts a*
8   *couple of slices of bacon on her plate and then looks up at her*
9   *mother.)* **You know one day, a hundred years from now, it**
10   **won't matter whether I went to school or not.** *(Picks up a slice*
11   *of bacon and takes a bite.)* **Yum. Good bacon.** *(Looks around*
12   *the table.)* **Yup. One hundred years from now, none of us will**
13   **be here anyway. What? It's true. So today, in the grand**
14   **scheme of things, is pretty insignificant one way or the**
15   **other. I mean whether I go to school or not. Please pass the**
16   **orange juice.** *(Takes the container and shakes it.)* **Thanks,**
17   **Carrie, it's empty.** *(Rolls her eyes and shakes her head.)* **So,**
18   **Mom, are you gonna give me a break today and let me stay**
19   **home? I'll clean the whole house. I'll ... oh, come on, Mom,**
20   **please!** *(Pushes plate away and puts her head on table*
21   *dejectedly then looks up.)* **Hey, why are you guys laughing?**
22   *(Covers her face in embarrassment.)* **Oh my gosh, it's Saturday!**

16. Laura Kelly's Diary

1   Hey, you guys, look what I have. Laura Kelly's diary.
2 *(Puts it behind her back.)* **Oh, no, no, no. I found it first. I'm**
3 **not handing this baby over to anybody. However, I will read**
4 **it to you if you're real nice. Yeah, OK, just have a seat over**
5 **there and put your money in my shoe** *(Slides off her sneaker).*
6 **Yes, I said money. Fifty cents each for the first page. Then**
7 **if you want to hear more, we'll talk. You know, we'll work**
8 **something out. Go ahead. Fifty cents each. If you don't want**
9 **to hear it, that's fine with me. Yeah, that's it, just pass the**
10 **shoe around, thank you very much. Good. Alright.** *(Looks in*
11 *shoe.)* **Looks like we're ready for page numero uno.** *(Opens*
12 *book with a sly smile and reads.)* **"Dear Diary, It's September**
13 **14th, the first day of school. I hope Johnny Rider is in all of**
14 **my classes."** *(Laughs.)* **Johnny Rider?! Johnny Rider doesn't**
15 **even know Laura Kelly is alive. OK, OK, I'll read. "Yesterday,**
16 **Mom took me shopping for some clothes. We had the usual**
17 **struggle over what I'd wear this year. I wanted to get some**
18 **really cool platform shoes. She said I could, but she also**
19 **bought me a pair of ballet flats that she liked. I told her that**
20 **I didn't want those shoes, but she insisted. I cried." She**
21 **cried? What? What a baby. Laura Kelly is an even bigger**
22 **dork than I thought. OK, OK, I'm reading. "I'm going**
23 **downstairs for breakfast now and then to the bus stop. I**
24 **hope Billie Forrest isn't there. I heard her parents bought**
25 **her a car, so I might be spared her obnoxious comments on**
26 **the bus this year." Ooooh, Billie! You're in Laura Kelly's**
27 **diary! I think you're gonna have to ride the bus tomorrow**
28 **just for fun and let me borrow your new car.** *(Laughs*

1   *hysterically.)* **OK! Shut up, I'm reading.** "Mom's yelling for
2   me to get downstairs, so for now, dear diary, farewell." Oh,
3   farewell dear diary. *(Laughing)* **OK, there's** more. "After
4   school, same day. Dear Diary, I am back home from school.
5   The first day of my sophomore year is over. Thank
6   goodness. What an awful day. Beebee Keaton is in all of my
7   classes and Johnny Rider is in none of them at all."
8   *(Chanting)* **Beebee, Beebee, Beebee.** *(Laughing)* **OK, OK.** "I
9   wish Johnny Rider did better in school. I know I could help
10 him if we were friends. Then we might have at least one
11 class together. Oh, well. Only in my dreams I guess. I can't
12 write much tonight because I have about five hours of
13 homework already. Ugh!" OK, that's the end of page one,
14 fifty more cents if you want to hear more. Yeah, I know, of
15 course it's boring. It's Laura Kelly's diary, right? You didn't
16 expect to hear about anything exciting, did you? No, you
17 cannot get your money back. That was not part of the deal!
18 OK, I'll read one more page, *(Puts on a phony voice.)* selected
19 randomly. OK, here we go *(Randomly picks out a page.)* "Dear
20 Diary, It's November 3rd, my birthday. Meredith Jones
21 totally ruined my day." Hey, that's me! *(Smiles and goes on*
22 *reading.)* "At school today, I had to get up in front of English
23 class and read my book report. I worked so hard on that,
24 but Meredith Jones sat in the back of the room and totally
25 made fun of everything I said and did." *(Laughing and*
26 *dancing around)* I did. I totally did. OK, OK. *(Phony voice*
27 *again)* Going on ... "Mrs. Carmichael can't hear very well, so
28 I'm not sure that she even knew, but even if she did she
29 probably wouldn't have done anything. Nobody knows what
30 to do with Meredith Jones. She's totally out of control."
31 *(Looks at the group and says in phony voice again)* That's rude.
32 True, but rude. Going on ... "I know I shouldn't feel sorry for
33 myself, but I did." Oh boo hoo, poor baby. "But, I really
34 wanted to feel good about something today and that book
35 report was my only chance. Of course, I know I shouldn't

1   hate Meredith." No, you should not. "I know I should forgive
2   her. She couldn't possibly know what I'm going through.
3   She couldn't possibly know that yesterday my mom found
4   out she has cancer." *(Freezes.)* I don't want to read anymore.
5   *(Hands the book to one of her friends.)* Here, you can have it.
6   No, I don't want it anymore. *(Dumps the change out of her*
7   *shoe.)* Take your money back, too. I was only joking. Who
8   wants to read Laura Kelly's stupid diary anyway.

17. Little White Lies

1   I hate little white lies. People say they're harmless, but
2   they're not. In fact, it's little white lies that have ruined my
3   life. I've told so many of them this year. It seemed the
4   easiest thing to do at the time. First little white lie? After we
5   moved to Harwick I was about to turn sixteen and should
6   have been getting my driver's license, but the truth is I'm
7   totally afraid of driving. It terrifies me. So I told everyone at
8   school that my mother was so strict that she wouldn't let
9   me drive until I'm eighteen. Why didn't I tell them the truth?
10 I thought they'd make fun of me. And they would have, of
11 course. I could have told them that I was in a really bad
12 accident when I was five, but they probably still wouldn't
13 have understood. They'd just be like, "Get thee to a
14 shrink." That's how they talk. My friends. Yeah, I hang out
15 with a really cool crowd. I like the friends I've made in
16 Harwick. They're the best. But I can't invite them over to my
17 house now, 'cause if I did, they'd meet my mom. Then
18 sooner or later the subject of driving would come up and
19 they'd be like, "Mrs. Lumpstorm, why won't you let Jessica
20 drive?" And she'd just never understand why I told a lie like
21 that. I mean, I've got the greatest mother in the world. So
22 you see, I can never invite my new friends over to my house
23 and that seems weird, right? So, I had to tell them that my
24 dad has multiple personality disorder and it's not safe for
25 anyone to come in our house in case he might be having an
26 episode. I sure hope he never finds out. I live in fear of that
27 day. So you see, little white lies, I think they're going to be
28 the death of me.

18. Say "Cheese"

1   It's not just a coincidence that I'm the chief yearbook
2   photographer, you know. I mean, I'm seriously talented. I
3   mean it. I'm really, really good. I'm not trying to brag. It's
4   just a gift. It's just in my blood. My DNA. Passed down
5   from my dad and his dad before him and probably his dad
6   before him I guess. Yeah, I'd say I've had a camera in my
7   hand about ninety-nine percent of the time since I was, oh,
8   about this big. *(Gestures to about the height of her knee.)* I've
9   even got a little photo studio in my house where I do
10   glamour shots. It's made me highly popular at school. Carol
11   Barnett, my neighbor, does the makeup. My mother, an
12   amateur costume designer at our community theater,
13   provides the wardrobe. It's a lot of fun and pretty lucrative,
14   too. Although, I have to say I do give all the girls a real deal.
15   Especially if they're from Perry High. I mean, if I charge them
16   an arm and a leg, they might as well go to the mall. I do
17   shoots outdoors, too, and I love to shoot animals. Oh, that
18   sounds terrible doesn't it. I mean with my camera, of
19   course. Puppies are an adorable subject. Well, babies are,
20   too. I mean, photography is really an art. It's so much more
21   than snapping a shot with your phone. It's *tres* complex if
22   you know what you're doing. And fortunately, I do. Last
23   night I went to the pizza parlor after our team won the
24   homecoming game and everybody there wanted me to get
25   them in a shot. They knew they'd have a good chance of
26   winding up in our school yearbook that way and looking
27   good, too. At times like that, though, I sometimes wish I'd
28   left my camera at home. I mean, I was so busy shooting last

1   night that I never even had a chance to eat. I ended up
2   taking a large pepperoni home. It's funny, but with me, I
3   guess everybody only thinks of one thing when they say,
4   "Cheese."

19. Ginger Snaps

1   *(Character named GINGER speaks.)* **"Can you please turn**
2   **that down! My eardrums are going to burst. I said ...** *(Walks*
3   *over to the stereo and turns it down.)* **I said, could you please**
4   **turn that down?** *(Walks back to the other side of the room to*
5   *attempt to study. Sarcastically)* **Thanks. Thanks, a lot.** *(Starts*
6   *to study and the music is turned back on even louder.)* **You are**
7   **such a jerk! Turn it off! Or, put your headphones on! I am**
8   **trying to study here.** *(Gets up in a huff and turns the stereo off*
9   *again.)* **What? Why don't I go to the library? Why don't you**
10   **go home? I don't know why you're here anyway. You are so**
11   **not into school. I swear, I don't know how I could possibly**
12   **get the worst roommate in the entire world, but somehow I**
13   **managed it. I mean, I was so excited about coming here but**
14   **if I have to go through the rest of the year with you as my**
15   **roommate, I'm going to lose my mind. I've told the**
16   **headmistress. She just said, "My goodness, you've only**
17   **been here a couple of months and you're already**
18   **complaining. You will learn, dear, that at Ryerson everyone**
19   **gets along." Funny, but she didn't seem to want to hear**
20   **anything negative about you. I don't suppose that could be**
21   **because your mother is, you know, like the most famous**
22   **pop star that ever lived. And if that weren't enough, your**
23   **father practically donated money enough to buy this whole**
24   **school. I'm here on scholarship, so nobody is worried about**
25   **me. Everybody knows that my parents probably couldn't buy**
26   **the doormat on your parents' doorstep, since it's probably**
27   **made out of solid gold. So look, I've got no other option but**
28   **to ask you nicely. Please, please let me study, here in this**

1   room, where I live. With you. Please. *(Her roommate gets up to*
2   *turn the stereo on.)* What are you doing? Stop right there. You
3   are not turning that back on again. I mean it. *(Her roommate*
4   *turns the stereo on full blast. GINGER gets up and marches over*
5   *to the stereo, picks it up, and stomps over to the window.)* I knew
6   that living on the fourth floor would come in handy one day.
7   *(Opens up the window, looks down below, and then throws the*
8   *stereo out and watches it hit the ground.)* Bam! *(Smiles and goes*
9   *back to her side of the room to study.)* What are you looking at?
10 Haven't you ever seen a Ginger snap? *(Imitating the*
11 *headmistress)* My goodness, you'll have to learn, dear. Why,
12 here at Ryerson, it happens all the time.

20. Post Op

1   *(Suppressing a giggle)* **Stop trying to make me laugh. I**
2   **mean it! Stop!** **'Cause it hurts, dummy. 'Cause I have**
3   **stitches, nitwit.** *(Holds sides. In between suppressed laughter)*
4   **Seriously, Scotty, if you don't stop, I'll ring for the nurse. I'll**
5   **ask her to make you leave. I'll never speak to you again.**
6   *(Taking a deep breath)* **OK, that's better. OK, you're not**
7   **allowed to talk unless you talk about something that's not**
8   **funny. I know how hard that is for you, being the class clown**
9   **and all that. I mean, I don't think I've ever had a**
10   **conversation with you when you weren't clowning around.**
11   **Seriously. You need to be serious for a change.** *(Lays back on*
12   *the hospital bed.)* **Otherwise you'll have to go. I really mean**
13   **it. If you can't be serious, you'll have to leave, or if you stay**
14   **you can't talk at all. I mean it. Uh, uh, no speaking. Really?**
15   **You've got something serious to say? Right. I don't believe**
16   **you. You wouldn't lie to me, would you? That's probably a**
17   **stupid question. If it would get a laugh you'd lie to me,**
18   **wouldn't you? You'll give me a million dollars if you make me**
19   **laugh? Gee, thanks. Why not make it five million dollars.**
20   **What? Are you suddenly Justin Bieber or something? OK,**
21   **OK, I believe you. I think. OK, go ahead. What is this**
22   **serious thing you have to say? Go on. What, has the cat got**
23   **your tongue? Scotty, you're driving me crazy. Now be nice**
24   **and say what you've got to say. I really want to know what's**
25   **on your mind. Go on, you've got a captive audience. I've just**
26   **had surgery and I'm not going anywhere. Am I gonna have**
27   **to guess? OK, you're driving me nuts. I'm gonna ring for the**
28   **nurse so that she can make you leave.** *(Starts to ring for the*

1   *nurse then freezes.)* **What? What did you just say? You love**
2   **me? You love me?** *(Starts to cry and holds her side.)* **Oh, no.**
3   **Scotty, it hurts when I cry, too. You're killing me, Scotty.**
4   **You really are. But,** *(Wiping her eyes)* **you wanna hear**
5   **something funny? I love you, too.**

21. Teenage Virus

1   You're new here so you probably haven't heard about the
2 school closure last year, right around Easter. The school
3 board tried to make everyone think they were just extending
4 spring break to be nice, but I know the truth. In fact most
5 people do. It was an outbreak of *(Looks around and then says*
6 *in a whisper.)* the Teenage Virus. I mean, it's not a secret.
7 It's just I don't want anyone to hear me 'cause they might
8 think it's happening again and if rumors spread they could
9 set off a school-wide panic, if you know what I mean. Well,
10 OK, it happened last year like I said. It was around Easter
11 and everybody was getting ready for spring break. All of a
12 sudden some of us noticed that the teachers were acting
13 pretty strange. Ms. Berger started taking out her hairbrush
14 in the middle of class and brushing her hair while we were
15 giving our oral reports. Then she called me up to the front
16 of the room and asked if I would take a note over to Mr. P
17 for her. Before I walked away, she whispered, "Don't let him
18 know it's from me." I thought that was weird, so when I got
19 out in the hall I opened it up. It was a love note signed,
20 "From your secret admirer." I thought, "This must be a
21 joke." But, I didn't want to give it to Mr. P, 'cause I thought
22 I'd get in trouble. So I just wandered around in the hall for
23 a minute, threw the note in the garbage and then went back
24 to class. Ms. Berger was in the middle of starting a talk on
25 the poetry of Wordsworth when I came in the door. She
26 stopped talking immediately and rushed over to me giggling
27 and whispered, "What did he say?" Everyone in the class
28 was staring at me. I said, "Um, he didn't say anything, Ms.

1 Berger," at which point she totally forgot herself and whined
2 loudly, "Oh, he doesn't like me, I just know it," then she
3 burst into tears. The rest of the day, girlfriend, went
4 downhill from there. All sorts of strange activities went on.
5 Teachers kissing in the hall. Mr. Bates sat in front of the
6 class chewing bubble gum the whole period. No, not just
7 chewing bubble gum, popping bubbles. At the end of the day
8 the Principal came on the intercom to make an
9 announcement, started laughing hysterically, and had to be
10 sent home. School was shut down the next day. Like I said,
11 they told us we were getting out early for spring break.
12 Getting extra days since we'd been such great kids all year.
13 Right. It was the Teenage Virus, that's what it was. The
14 Teenage Virus. Turns out Ms. Berger caught it on a flight
15 back home from visiting her relatives and she passed it
16 around the whole faculty before anyone figured it out.
17 Luckily there's a cure and a vaccination, so I don't think it
18 will ever happen again. Not here anyway, at Jefferson High.
19 I say "thank goodness." I don't ever want to see Mr.
20 McGuire and Ms. Kettle making out in the hall again.

22. I Wish This Day Would Last Forever

1   I wish this day would last forever. It's my last day of
2 freedom. Oh, you know, school's starting. No, not
3 tomorrow, but I go back home tomorrow. Naw, I don't live
4 here. I just spend the summer here with my dad. Then I go
5 back home when it's time for the school year to start again.
6 So my plane leaves in the morning. Yeah, I'm sad. I'm sad
7 to see the summer end, but more than that, I'm sorry to
8 leave my friends. I mean, it's weird because I am excited
9 about seeing my friends at home, too, but there are kids
10 here that I've known since I was about three years old. Of
11 course, when my parents got divorced, when I was eight, I
12 left to live with my mom in Texas about a million miles away.
13 So I've only seen these kids in the summer, but I've seen
14 them every summer. So we're really close, you know. With
15 most of them, their whole family is like my family. And they
16 sort of feel that way about me and my dad, too. It's like the
17 kids on my dad's street are just one big family. I don't have
18 that at home. Most of my friends, well, really all of my
19 friends are at school. So this place is really special to me.
20 It's funny, too, because every year I worry. I think, "I wonder
21 if I've changed a lot? Have they changed a lot? Will we still
22 get along?" And it's true we do change every year and it's a
23 little weird at first. When I first get here. But it doesn't take
24 long. I'd say about a day at the most. Then it's just like we
25 were never ever apart. So yeah, I don't want to see today
26 end. But, unfortunately, it will. It's like my mom always
27 says, "That's the funny thing about time. It won't stop for
28 you or anybody else. Time marches on." But still, I hate to
29 see it go.

23. Suddenly Sidney

1   My life was so perfect in every way. And then suddenly,
2 there was Sidney. Who would think that a little squirt about
3 twenty inches long and eight pounds eleven ounces would
4 bring so much chaos into my life? I had no idea. In fact,
5 when my stepmom, Sandra, and my dad told me they were
6 expecting, I was ecstatic. When I heard it was a little
7 brother? I was even more ecstatic. And Sidney is adorable,
8 but he loves to cry. At night. When I have to go to school
9 the next day. It's been pretty hard adjusting to that. Plus,
10 Sandra has very definite ideas about raising Sidney and
11 frankly they are cramping my style. Like what? OK, like
12 when he cries at night, she says, "Let him cry. I don't want
13 him to think he can make this a habit and that every time
14 he cries he'll get his way." I'm like, "Hello, I have to go to
15 school tomorrow. Can we worry about breaking Sidney's bad
16 habits some other day?" Sandra just looks at me and says
17 "So you're saying I should not discipline my son so that you
18 can get a good night's sleep?" That didn't sound right to
19 me. Disciplining? I can't even believe her sometimes. Since
20 when do you discipline an infant? That's so harsh. Well,
21 Sidney is lucky 'cause I'm on his side. Sometimes at night
22 when I hear him just starting to cry, I'll go in and pick him
23 up really fast before Sandra wakes up and hears him. Then
24 we sit in the rocker and I'll sing very quietly to him or tell
25 him stories. Sometimes I'll tell him all about stuff that's
26 happening at school. He's a really good listener. And even
27 though that sort of night makes me really tired the next day,
28 I don't really care. I love Sidney so much. I never knew how

1   wonderful having a little brother would be. I mean, here I am
2   an only child for fifteen years, and then suddenly ... Sidney.

24. My Best Friend

1   My best friend Carrie can be a jerk sometimes.
2   Seriously. Well, actually, she can be more than a jerk. She
3   can be pretty rotten. But we're still friends. I guess we've
4   just been friends for so long and it's just a comfortable
5   friendship now. Most of the time anyway. Lately it's been a
6   little bit uncomfortable, though. I guess I'm growing up and
7   getting a conscience. So when Carrie pulls her little stunts I
8   still laugh on the outside, but on the inside I'm just ... a
9   mess. A mess of guilt. I never say anything to Carrie
10   because I've never ever argued with her. Not seriously.
11   Confronting Carrie just wouldn't feel right. But it doesn't feel
12   right going along with some of her shenanigans lately,
13   either. Oh, well, I might as well stop beating around the
14   bush and just tell you what she's done now. *(Takes a deep*
15   *breath.)* You have to swear first that you won't tell a living
16   soul. I would just die if Carrie found out I was talking behind
17   her back. OK, well, a few weeks ago a bunch of us girls were
18   planning a trip to Florida for spring break. We were so
19   excited. It was going to be Mary Web, Sara Gibbs, Kathy
20   Turner, and, of course, Carrie and me. We had permission to
21   take Carrie's mother's car and there was just enough room
22   for the five of us. Well, as it got really, really close to the day
23   we would leave, Carrie met some goofball guy named
24   Rooster. She met him, appropriately, at the Goofy Golf near
25   the river. Well, according to Carrie it was love at first sight
26   and he just had to go with us on the trip. Carrie and I were
27   at Pop's 48 Flavors when she told me this, sharing a
28   Kitchen Sink Colossal Banana Split. I said, "Well maybe he

1 can go with us next year, 'cause your mom's car is full, isn't
2 it?" Carrie just got a grin and said, "Not anymore." I was
3 like, "What do you mean?" She says, "I just called Kathy
4 Turner and told her that she can't come." My jaw dropped
5 and a piece of banana slid out on a stream of chocolate
6 sauce. "You did?" I said in disbelief. "What did you tell her?"
7 Carrie says, "I just told her the truth. Rooster is in and you
8 are out. *(Laughing)* She was really ticked off." I wanted to
9 say something like "That was so mean!" or "If Kathy doesn't
10 go, I'm not going." But, my lips just wouldn't let the words
11 come out. Finally, on the way home, I got up the nerve to
12 ask, "Why did you pick Kathy?" Carrie looks at me and says,
13 "Well, I didn't want her to come because she's prettier than
14 me. I really like Rooster and I don't want anything messing
15 that up." I wanted to call Kathy later that night to see how
16 she was, but I didn't have the nerve. I'm sure she felt
17 horrible. She had been so excited. I think she had already
18 packed. I wanted to tell her the reason so that at least she'd
19 know why. At least she'd know that it wasn't because we
20 didn't like her. It was just because Carrie was afraid that
21 Rooster would like her too much. Yeah, my best friend Carrie
22 is a jerk and sometimes I worry. Does that make me a jerk
23 by association? Yeah, I know it does. And I'm not sure I
24 want to be one anymore.

25. Green

1   Everybody's trying to go green these days, right? Well,
2   my parents are no exception to that rule. In fact, if they got
3   any greener they'd look like broccoli. Well, Mom would look
4   like broccoli and Dad would definitely resemble a celery
5   stick. For real though. They are so green it's embarrassing.
6   Last year they were in our town paper. On the front page.
7   Sitting in trees. They were doing it for a good cause. They
8   didn't want the trees to be cut down. I love trees as much
9   as the next girl, but it was still embarrassing. Especially
10   when they dragged them kicking and screaming out of the
11   trees on the evening news. That video ended up going viral
12   of course. And me? I ended up being the laughing stock of
13   the school once again. Yeah, it's been happening all my life.
14   Stupid stuff like that. Stuff that I should be proud of, of
15   course, if I had any character. But unfortunately, I
16   apparently have none. Because I just want to crawl under a
17   rock and die when something like that happens. My green
18   parents are not just embarrassing. They're a little bit
19   irritating, too. They won't ever use any unnecessary energy.
20   Like for air conditioning when the summer gets boiling hot.
21   So I sit in my bedroom at night in a lather of sweat counting
22   the days until winter. Me? I'd rather freeze than swelter any
23   day. And freeze I do when the temperature drops outside.
24   We wouldn't want to waste any energy using our central
25   heat, would we, Mom and Dad? Of course not. So yeah,
26   even though it's cool to be green and by rights I totally
27   should be green if you think of my DNA, I'm not. I am not
28   green. I don't want to be green. I will never be green. Well, I

1   take that back. Whenever I see a kid with normal parents
2   who don't sit in trees, I'm green ... green with envy, that is.
3   Totally.

26. The Brat

1   *(Raising hand to be called on)* **Ms. Henderson, do you**
2   **think that saying about teachers is true? You know, "Those**
3   **who can, do. Those who can't, teach."** *(Turns around to the*
4   *boy seated behind her.)* **I am not being rude. I am just asking**
5   **a question.** *(Back to Ms. Henderson)* **I mean, no offense, Ms.**
6   **Henderson, but that's what my stepfather Frank always**
7   **says. And everybody has a right to their own opinion, don't**
8   **they? What does Frank do? He's a lawyer. Yeah, he went to**
9   **school. I think. Yeah, so maybe he does owe something to**
10   **his teachers, I guess. Yeah, they probably taught him to**
11   **read and all that. They sure didn't teach him any manners,**
12   **though. He's so rude.** *(Turns around to the kid behind her.)* **I**
13   **do not take after him. He's my stepfather, you idiot.** *(To Ms.*
14   *Henderson)* **I'm sorry, Ms. Henderson. I'll be quiet.** *(Sits*
15   *quietly for a moment, then to the boy behind her)* **Hey, stop**
16   **kicking my chair. Yes, you did. Ms. Henderson, he kicked**
17   **my chair. You want me to move? He kicked my chair and**
18   **you want me to move.** *(To boy behind her)* **Yeah, you move,**
19   **go ahead. Good idea. What did you just say? Ms.**
20   **Henderson, he just said that he's happy to move away from**
21   **me. That's very insulting, don't you think? Sure, I said I'd**
22   **be quiet, but that was before he kicked my chair.** *(Quiet for*
23   *a moment, then)* **Ms. Henderson, what page are we supposed**
24   **to be doing? I know you told us half an hour ago, but I**
25   **forgot. It's hard to concentrate in here. Why? It smells. Yeah,**
26   **it smells like rotten eggs or something. Did somebody have**
27   **something stinky for lunch? OK, OK, Ms. Henderson, I'll be**
28   **quiet. You don't need to send me to the office. I'll stop**

1   **disrupting the class.** *(Looks around the room. Sarcastically)*
2   **Sorry, class. I won't talk anymore.** *(Looks up at Ms. Henderson*
3   *and zips her lips and pretends to throw away the key. Turns the*
4   *pages in her book and picks up her pencil. Starts lightly tapping*
5   *on the desk and then starts humming along with the beat. Looks*
6   *up as Ms. Henderson stands over her desk. Starts to speak.)* **I'm**
7   **...** *(Covers her mouth as she remembers she's zipped her lips. Tries*
8   *to talk through her lips like a ventriloquist.)* **I'm sorry, Ms.**
9   **Henderson. That was very disruptive.** *(Now speaking at Ms.*
10 *Henderson's request)* **I said, "I'm sorry Ms. Henderson; that**
11 **was very disruptive." Huh? I'm leaving? Where am I going,**
12 **on a cruise?** *(Laughs at her own joke. Then whining)* **To the**
13 **office? Why? That's so unfair. You didn't give me a chance.**
14 **Alright fine.** *(Picks up her things and stomps to the door. Then*
15 *turns to the class, grinning.)* **Later losers!** *(Exits.)*

27. Bad to the Bone

1   Hey, look what I found in your mom's purse ... *(Holds up*
2   *the money.)* One hundred smackeroos! What? Don't worry,
3   she didn't see me. She's asleep on the couch. Put it back?
4   Are you kidding? You just said you needed a new pair of
5   sneakers, didn't you? Well, here you go. Hey! I'm trying to
6   do something nice for you here. I'm trying to be a friend.
7   And what do I get for it? A lot of lip. Fine, fine. *(Throws the*
8   *money at her.)* You put it back. What did you invite me over
9   here for anyway? This is so boring. We don't have anything
10   in common anymore. You're no fun anymore. It's over. It's
11   done and I'm leaving. What's done? Our friendship. That's
12   what's done. I don't know what they did to you at that
13   summer camp, but it's like I don't even know you anymore.
14   No, it's more like I don't want to know you. Miss Goody-Two-
15   Shoes. That's what you are. Well, I'm taking my stuff and
16   I'm leaving. You can have your stupid swimming pool and
17   you can watch your stupid movie yourself. I've got better
18   things to do. Like have a life. Like hang with some cool
19   people I know. Geez, you don't even smoke anymore. What's
20   with that? You know what, you'll start up again. Just wait
21   and see. I'll see you in a few months and you'll be standing
22   on the corner puffin' away and hanging with some jerk when
23   you could have been hanging with me. You'll go back to all
24   your old ways when you get bored stiff with your new life and
25   you'll be begging me to come hang with you, but you can
26   just forget about that. You made your choice, Miss Perfect.
27   But it won't stick. You'll see. You're just as bad as you used
28   to be. You're bad to the bone, just like me.

28. Sorry Is As Sorry Does

1   *(Putting down a letter she's been reading)* **This is supposed**
2 **to be an apology?! This is pathetic. What does he think?**
3 **That he can just act like the biggest idiot in the universe**
4 **and treat me like garbage, then write a stupid note like this**
5 **and be forgiven. Words! That's all it is. A bunch of**
6 **meaningless words. My grandma used to say, "Sorry is as**
7 **sorry does." She was right. She was totally right. If he's**
8 **sorry he should act like he's sorry. He should act like the**
9 **kind of guy he could be. The kind of guy he should be. But**
10 **he won't. He'll just think this letter will make everything**
11 **better and we'll be going out again. Then he can just keep**
12 **on being the same old Dan. The same old guy who makes**
13 **me feel like I'm about as big as a flea most of the time. Well,**
14 **it's not going to happen. I guess I'm not as dumb as he**
15 **thinks I am. Or maybe, it just took awhile for me to get**
16 **smarter. I must not have been too bright to go out with him**
17 **in the first place, right? Yeah, everybody makes mistakes,**
18 **but I wish I hadn't. He just wasted my whole senior year.**
19 **Boy, he thinks he's sorry, but the only one who's really sorry**
20 **is me.**

29. Choices

1   I hate making decisions. Making choices. Even on little
2 things like, "Where do you want to go for lunch?" My
3 standard answer is, "I don't know. Wherever you want to go,
4 I guess." But this summer a really big decision has to be
5 made by me. I have a choice. I was invited, well kind of
6 begged, by my dad to come live with him and his new wife.
7 See, my dad has always had a really small one bedroom
8 apartment and where I lived, which is with my mom, was
9 never questioned. But now he got married to a very wealthy
10 lady. They live on a beautiful ranch with a bunch of horses.
11 Beautiful horses. And their house is amazing. They have five
12 bedrooms and an amazing swimming pool with a water
13 slide. Their neighborhood has fantastic schools and well, I
14 could go on and on. The only thing is ... I love my mom. I
15 love my dad too, but I've always lived with my mom. We live
16 in an apartment, but it's nice. I can live with my dad and
17 have it made, but I love my mom. I've always lived with her.
18 I couldn't leave her alone. She says, "Don't think about me
19 when you make this decision. This is about what's best for
20 you." Some of my friends think I'd be crazy not to jump at
21 the chance. They're like, "Horses and your own swimming
22 pool? It's like a dream come true." But, the whole thing
23 makes me really sad. If I go with my dad, I know it will break
24 my mom's heart. If I tell my dad no, he'll think I don't love
25 him. What would you do?

30. BFF Showdown

1   Oh my gosh! Dad, are you home? Dad? Oh, Dad! I won!
2 We won! The BFF Showdown.
3   What's a BFF Showdown? Dad! I told you all about it
4 yesterday! Don't you ever listen to me? OK, OK, I'll tell you
5 again. They had this contest at school called the BFF
6 Showdown. You know, just for fun. It was sponsored by the
7 student council or something. So anyway, it was like that
8 old show where couples — husbands and wives — would
9 have to answer questions about each other for a prize. Yeah,
10 yeah, that's the one. So this was like that game show, but
11 different 'cause it was about BFFs. Best Friends Forever.
12 Which, of course, is Tiffany and me. So ... we competed and
13 we won! We won two free tickets to the One Direction
14 concert. *(Jumping up and down)* Do you believe it?! I am so
15 psyched. Oh, Dad, we were amazing. We knew absolutely
16 everything about each other. We got every single answer
17 right. Then it came down to a tie between us and two other
18 BFFs, Cindy Shoe and Millie Estevez and Brian Green and
19 Elizabeth Walters. Yes, Dad, a boy and girl can be best
20 friends. It's the twenty-first century, you know. Not like
21 things were when you and Abraham Lincoln went to school.
22 So anyway, we got down to the tiebreaker, which was to
23 name your BFFs most embarrassing experience. I was
24 soooo nervous. The whole school was watching. Yeah, they
25 broadcast us on every classroom TV. So, here we were with
26 the whole school watching and it all came down to me. Yeah,
27 you see, every other player got the answer wrong. I was the
28 last one and if I didn't get it right it would have been another

1 tie and another question and then who knows what might
2 have happened. So I'm sitting there and I'm thinking, what
3 was it? What was Tiffany's most embarrassing experience?
4 Well, there have been a lot of them, I know, so it wasn't
5 easy, but I was pretty sure I had it. So I said, "Tiffany's
6 most embarrassing experience was the first time she had to
7 go to the lingerie department and buy a bra." And I was
8 right! The whole room burst into applause. Tiffany turned
9 red as a beet, but needless to say, she was happy, too.
10 Later we just laughed and laughed at the whole experience
11 and said we'd both play again. Next time though, Tiffany
12 says her most embarrassing experience will be the whole
13 school knowing about her most embarrassing experience. I
14 was like, geez, Tiffany, it's not a big deal. I mean at least I
15 didn't tell them about the time she ... you know.

31. Election Fraud

1   Maria, if I tell you something will you promise never to
2   tell another living soul? You swear? OK. I know something
3   about the school election and I don't know what to do.
4   Well, you know how the results were just announced
5   yesterday and the winning ticket was Bobby and Lisa? Well,
6   I think it should have been Lance and Rodney. Yeah. I mean,
7   I know it should have been Lance and Rodney. You see, I
8   was in the room when the votes were being counted and I
9   saw something that I wish I'd never seen. I saw the student
10   council treasurer, yeah C.J., do something that I just
11   couldn't believe. When no one was looking, or when he
12   thought no one was looking, he put a handful of ballots in
13   his right pocket and replaced them with a handful of ballots
14   from his left pocket. I know, I know, I should have said
15   something, but I was in shock. I didn't know what to do. So
16   then, at the end of the counting, it turns out that Bobby and
17   Lisa won by three votes. They only had three votes more
18   than Lance and Rodney. I just know that those votes in
19   C.J.'s pocket would have, you know, changed the results.
20   No, I can't be sure that they were for Bobby and Lisa, but
21   I'd bet you a million dollars. Now the results have been
22   announced and I feel terrible. What should I do?

32. Cheerleader Number Five, In Miranda's Words

1   This is weird. Shiloh and I try out for cheerleading every
2 year and we both never make it. This year, for some weird
3 reason, I made it. I am Cheerleader Number Five.
4   Thanks. Yeah, it's great. It is. But it's weird, because
5 Shiloh didn't make it. She tried to make a joke out of it
6 afterwards saying, "Guess I'm just Cheerleader Number
7 Zero." But I could see the tears in her eyes. It totally sucks.
8 I mean, every year we had each other to lean on when we
9 didn't make the cut. Now Shiloh doesn't even want to talk
10 about it. I can't blame her. Would you? It must be horrible
11 for her. It's like, we've always done everything together our
12 whole lives and now I'm on a different path. Going a different
13 direction. Already I've got cheerleader meetings and
14 practice. It's like a whole other world that she won't be a
15 part of. And next year, when we actually cheer at games,
16 she'll be sitting up there in the stands. Where we used to sit
17 together. I almost wish I hadn't made it. I almost wish I
18 hadn't been good. But somehow I miraculously was. I felt it
19 that day. I was spot on in every cheer. I could see Shiloh
20 screwing up out of the corner of my eye. Maybe I should
21 have tried to screw up too. Maybe this whole cheerleading
22 thing will be a big mistake. My mom thinks it's great. I think
23 she just wanted to tell her friends that I made the squad. I
24 think I usually just embarrass her. Her friends probably
25 think I'm a dork. Now they'll have to think twice. Dorks
26 don't make cheerleader, right? Yeah, right. I say, once a
27 dork always a dork. And proud of it too. I may be
28 Cheerleader Number Five, but inside I'm still the same
29 person I was, and always will be.

33. Cheerleader Number Five, in Shiloh's Words

1   This was the worst week of my life. On Monday I found
2   out that I didn't make the cheerleading squad once again.
3   What's worse? My best friend Miranda made it. I know I
4   should be happy for her. But please. Put yourself in my
5   shoes. Would you be? Miranda and I have always been
6   inseparable. As a matter of fact, we've tried out for
7   cheerleading every year together. And together, we were
8   soundly rejected. It was almost fun getting rejected when
9   we were like a team. We consoled each other over ice cream
10   sundaes. But this year, Miranda rose above me and made
11   the cut. Now I haven't seen her all week. She's either in
12   cheerleading meetings or cheerleading practice. At night,
13   her mom's been taking her to the mall and buying her all
14   these new clothes. It's like she's suddenly proud of her
15   when she wasn't before. Which I think is rude. Why should
16   Miranda being a cheerleader make such a difference to her
17   mom? Cheerleading is just for fun, right? It's not rocket
18   science. It's not like she made Honor Society or won the
19   school essay contest. My mom says cheerleading is a waste
20   of time. Anyway, I don't really care that I haven't seen
21   Miranda. I've got plenty of other friends. I've just been
22   neglecting them for a long time. You know, foolishly
23   spending all my time with Miranda. Only to get dumped in
24   the end for the cheerleading squad. Oh, well, you live and
25   learn, right? Yeah, I've learned a lot. I'm not even going to
26   the games next year. I think if I had to watch Miranda
27   cheering, I'd throw up. She didn't have to try so hard at
28   tryouts. She never said she really, seriously wanted to

1 cheer. I thought we were just trying out for fun.
2   Guess Miranda's Cheerleader Number Five, and I'm just
3 Dork Number One.

34. Grocery Shopping 101

1   Hey, that must be my brother Tom with the groceries.
2   He's so happy he got his new car. He's all grown up and
3   independent now. Offering to go get the groceries this week
4   so Mom doesn't have to. Hey, Tom. How were things at the
5   store? Awesome. So, let's see the bag. What did you get?
6   *(Looks in the bag.)* **What's this? Is this a joke? Tom, there's**
7   five boxes of macaroni in here and a bunch of cheese. Yeah,
8   macaroni and cheese is great, but you did get something
9   else, didn't you? You didn't? You didn't know what to get
10 'cause you don't cook? Well, you may not cook, but you eat,
11 don't you? You know that you don't eat macaroni and
12 cheese for breakfast, right? Well, there you go. You should
13 have gotten some eggs and bacon. Or how about some
14 cereal and milk? Tom! You'd better take me to the store so
15 we can fix this. Yeah, we do need to go. Otherwise Mom's
16 gonna have a fit. Come on, Mr. Grown-Up–and-Independent.
17 It'll be Grocery Shopping 101.

35. Minus Me

1   I've been made fun of for the last time. I'm quitting the
2   Outdoor Club. Yeah, I am serious. I don't like the way you
3   guys have been treating me at all. Nope. I don't. Yeah, I
4   know, I know, I'm quitting right before our annual camping
5   trip. I know. And yeah, it's a real shame. I'm gonna miss out
6   on soooo much. Yep, I'll miss out on all the fun. First of all,
7   I'll miss out on that long fume-ridden ride in Mrs. Berry's
8   old, broken-down van. Then I'll miss out on putting up the
9   tent. That's always a blast. And boy, will I miss out on using
10   a pinecone instead of TP. Yeah, it's sad all right. It's a
11   wonder I'm not bawling my eyes out right now. How will I
12   survive being here at home in the air conditioning when you
13   guys are all sweltering in the heat? Getting eaten by
14   mosquitoes. How envious I will be. Yeah, I'll just sit around
15   and think about how much fun it was last year and how
16   great it was to come home covered in poison ivy. Geez, I'm
17   sorry, but I've decided that in spite of all the fun I could have
18   had, based on the way you all have been acting, you're just
19   gonna have to go on the annual camping trip minus me.

36. Two Burgers, Two Fries, and a Little Romance

1   We didn't like each other at all at first. Well, at least I
2   definitely didn't like him. Instinctively. He was standing in
3   front of me squirting ketchup into about fifty little cups. You
4   know, those little white cups they use for ketchup at the Big
5   Blue Burger House on Fremont Street. Well, it was really
6   irritating me. I just wanted to get a little bit of ketchup for
7   my fries and he didn't even seem to notice that I was
8   standing there waiting. Finally, I said, "Excuse me, but do
9   you think I could possibly butt in and get just a little bit of
10   ketchup before you hog it all?" He was totally taken off
11   guard. I don't think he'd ever had a girl talk to him like that
12   before. You know, they all probably just batted their
13   eyelashes and swooned, seeing as he's so cute and all that.
14   But not me. I let him have it. And I don't think he liked it.
15   However, I definitely made an impression on him. He
16   stepped back and let me squirt my ketchup. So I did and
17   then I went back to my table. A little while later, I'm sitting
18   there eating my burger and fries and I could feel someone
19   staring at me. I looked over by the window and it was him.
20   He was with some girl with pigtails and a cheerleading
21   outfit. Of course she was super cute, but at that point,
22   sister, he only had eyes for me. But I just looked the other
23   way. I was not interested. Not at that point, anyway.
24   However, about a week passed and I got hungry for some
25   fries and a double-decker burger with bacon, onions, and
26   cheese, so I stopped at the Big Blue Burger on my way home
27   from school. And as fate would have it, guess who I bumped
28   into while I was waiting in line? Yup. The King of Ketchup

1   himself. Well, actually he bumped into me. He walked right
2   up to me and said, "If I buy you lunch will you let me cut
3   in?" I turned around and there wasn't a single soul behind
4   me in line. That made me laugh in spite of myself. I said,
5   "Where's Pom-Pom Penelope?" He said, "Don't know and
6   don't want to know." So, I let him buy me lunch. And we've
7   been dating ever since. Now I know that not everyone can
8   find true love at the Big Blue Burger, but ... that's where it
9   happened for me.

37. What If

1   Did you ever think about how technology has changed
2 the world? I mean sure, we've grown up with it so it's no big
3 deal, but just think about literature and history and how
4 things would have been different if the folks way back when
5 had the technology we've got today. An example? Well ...
6 OK. What if they had cell phones back in Shakespeare's
7 day? Would Romeo have texted Juliet? I'm sure he probably
8 would have, right? And that would have totally, seriously
9 changed the whole play. Think about it, it's true. With cell
10 phones, even though their families were feuding, Romeo and
11 Juliet could have talked to each other all day and night and
12 nobody would have been the wiser. And at the end of the
13 play, that last scene, well, I won't say anything about it in
14 case you haven't read it yet. But believe me, technology
15 would have totally ruined that story. Or how about "Gone
16 with the Wind?" Or "The Wizard of Oz?" Dorothy would have
17 probably pulled out her cell and called Auntie Em to tell her
18 she was on another planet or something. Or she might have
19 used her GPS to get back home. Who cares about the yellow
20 brick road or clicking your ruby slippers when you have a
21 GPS right? Anyway, I think it's fun to think about, don't
22 you? Yeah, I think as a writer those are my two favorite
23 words. What if.

38. My Big Pimple

1   *(Covering nose with one hand)* **This is a disaster! I have an**
2   **audition today and I woke up this morning with a gigantic**
3   **pimple on my nose. So what? Did you say, "So what?" I'll**
4   **tell you what! This could have been my big break, bozo! This**
5   **could have meant a national commercial! Yeah! As in**
6   *beaucoup* **bucks! That means a lot of money, idiot! No, it is**
7   **as bad as I'm saying it is. I am not exaggerating. No, I do**
8   **not want to show you! No, you'll just laugh. You'll just**
9   **make things worse. Oh, OK. You promise not to laugh? OK,**
10   **well. Stand over here, so they won't see. Them.** *(Points to the*
11   *audience with other hand.)* **I don't know who they are, but**
12   **they're staring at me. OK, yeah over here.** *(Turns to kid at her*
13   *side and uncovers nose very quickly and then covers it back up.*
14   *Looks back out front with embarrassment and shame, and then*
15   *glances back at kid.)* **Get off the floor. Stop laughing. Stop**
16   **rolling on the floor and laughing. You are such a jerk. You**
17   **are ...** *(Exasperated, gives up.)* **oh, who cares. Go ahead and**
18   **laugh. I would too. If it was on your nose, not mine. Oh, well,**
19   **I guess I'll just have to try to cover it up. I hope they don't**
20   **do a close-up. Maybe I should just put a Band-Aid on it and**
21   **say I broke it or something. No, I don't think they'll like that**
22   **either. Well, the title of my diary entry tonight is probably**
23   **not going to be "My Big Break." Unfortunately, it will**
24   **probably be "My Big Pimple."**

39. Mysteriously Good Pizza

1   *(Eating a slice of pizza)* **Oh, this is soooo good. I mean,**
2   **seriously, this has got to be the best pizza I've ever had. You**
3   **didn't really make this yourself, did you? The taste! The**
4   **flavor! It's ... it's incredible.** *Fantastico! Delizioso!* **I mean it,**
5   **Jennifer. I've been all over the world with my parents and**
6   **wherever I am, whenever I can, I get pizza. This pizza beats**
7   **anything I've ever had. The only pizza that I can ever**
8   **remember even getting remotely close to this one was in**
9   **Naples, Italy. It was a restaurant called La Vera Pizza, which**
10 **literally means the real pizza, and I'll never forget it. But this**
11 **one? I mean it. If you had a contest with expert chefs**
12 **judging, I swear they'd pick your pizza over the pizza from**
13 **La Vera Pizza. Up until today, I thought that was the best**
14 **pizza in the world. What in this world did you put in the**
15 **sauce? Oh, come on, please, please tell me. I promise I**
16 **won't tell a soul. You can whisper it in my ear just in case**
17 **any pizza spies in the area can possibly hear.** *(Leans over so*
18 *that Jennifer can whisper in her ear then pulls back in horror.)*
19 **Gross! Agh! You're joking right? Oh, gag me with a spoon.**
20 **Jennifer, I wish I'd never asked. That is disgusting. You're**
21 **joking, right? You are? You are.** *(Sighs with relief.)* **Oh, that**
22 **was not funny. That was soooo not funny. Oh my gosh, I**
23 **believed you. I totally believed you.** *(Laughing in spite of*
24 *herself)* **You make a great pizza Jennifer, but you totally just**
25 **freaked me out. Does this mean you're not going to tell me**
26 **what's in the pizza sauce? Ever? Yeah, that's what I thought.**
27 **OK, no worries. I will accept that your secret ingredients are**
28 **to remain a mystery. Forever. Believe me, I'll never ask you**
29 **again.**

40. Practice Will Make Perfect?

1   Stop laughing at me! Stop laughing at how bad I am and
2 help me to learn. Margo. Get a grip. You said you were
3 coming over here to teach me to dance, not to make me feel
4 like a clown. OK, I'll try it again, but you have to promise
5 not to laugh. OK, so show me again one more time. *(Watches*
6 *her friend do the dance step.)* OK. Great. I think I've got it
7 now. How's this? *(Does a ridiculous dance move then spins*
8 *around.)* Like that, right? Hey, you said you wouldn't laugh.
9 What? What was so funny? I did it just like you! Yes, I did.
10 OK, maybe that one's too hard. Can't you give me
11 something easier I could do? Margo, this is serious! I've got
12 to go to the sophomore dance this Friday with Gary. That
13 gives me exactly three whole days to learn how to dance.
14 OK, OK, I'll try harder. Just show me something easy.
15 *(Watches her friend.)* OK, OK. I can do that. Watch. *(Does*
16 *another absolutely ridiculous dance move.)* So? That was good,
17 right? Margo? I just need some practice. OK, OK. I'll
18 practice this move all night and we'll meet again tomorrow.
19 OK? *(Starts doing ridiculous move again.)* Thanks, Margo. See
20 you tomorrow. Bye!

41. Good News and Bad News

1   I have some good news and some bad news. The good
2 news is Ted Learner finally asked me out. Too cool, right? I
3 know, I know. I'm so excited. The bad news? He asked me
4 to go bungee jumping. Of course I said yes. No, I didn't tell
5 him I'm deathly afraid of heights. No, we didn't talk about
6 that at all. It was all, "Do you want to go out with me? Can
7 I get your number?" kind of talk. Nothing about our greatest
8 phobias in the universe. Oh my gosh! What am I going to
9 do? I can't tell him I won't do it. He might change his mind
10 and not want to go out with me at all. This is like a really
11 good dream with a really bad twist. Hey, you didn't put him
12 up to this did you? Why are you smiling? You wouldn't do
13 that! Would you? OK, OK, so I'm being paranoid. It's just,
14 how weird is this? Who asks someone to go bungee jumping
15 on their first date? Isn't a typical first date to the movies or
16 something like that? Isn't this whole thing a little extreme?
17 I swear, I wonder if someone told him that I'm afraid of
18 heights and he's putting me to the test. I don't know. Maybe
19 I should just call him up and tell him. Oh, I'm so confused.
20 Help me out here. What would you do?

42. Bikini Season

1   Well, it's that time of year again when everyone's hitting
2   the beach. Yup. Bikini season. Yesterday Gail and I went to
3   the mall to try on bathing suits. What a disaster. Yeah, it
4   was totally, completely depressing. How depressing was it?
5   Well, we were both really sorry we didn't join a gym when
6   we had the chance last year. It was horrible. I must have
7   tried on about fifty bikinis. Then I decided that was useless
8   and just started looking at one piece bathing suits, but that
9   wasn't any better. And Gail? Well, if I told you how she
10 looked in the bathing suits she tried on, I wouldn't be much
11 of a friend. So let's just say, "No comment." It's OK. After
12 we left the mall we did something to totally cheer ourselves
13 up. We went straight over to the ice cream shop and each of
14 us got an enormous, colossal hot fudge sundae. It worked.
15 We felt much better after that. I figure, I can still wear my
16 old bathing suit whenever or if ever I go to the beach this
17 summer. And by not getting a new bathing suit, I'll have a
18 lot more money for my ice cream habit. Hey, you got to go
19 with the flow, right?

43. Is It You?

1   Is the camera on? OK. *(Smiles.)* Hi, Billy. Mindy here, in
2   sunny Southern California. You asked me to tell you about
3   myself, Billy, so some friends are helping me make this
4   video. I hope you like it. OK, so some of the things you
5   wanted to know about were ... *(Looks at notecard.)* my
6   favorite vacation. My dream vacation. What I want to be.
7   Who would I consider a hero. And last but not least, how
8   would I describe my ideal guy. Well, those are all great
9   topics, by the way. And I hope I can answer them for you
10 without boring you too much. Let's see. I'll start with my
11 favorite vacation. That's a hard one because my family and
12 I have taken so many great vacations. We usually take a few
13 each year. We take them when school's out of course, so we
14 go somewhere each summer, winter, and spring break. I
15 know I'm very fortunate to be able to do that. My parents
16 own their own business and can pretty much name their
17 own schedules, so ... I'm getting off topic here. Sorry. So,
18 my favorite vacation is slightly difficult to choose, but I
19 guess I'd have to say any of our family trips to Chicago.
20 There is just something about that city. Have you ever
21 been? If not, I think you definitely should go. We had so
22 much fun there in the summer after seventh grade. My
23 cousins went with us and we all went to Navy Pier. They
24 have a Ferris wheel and boat rides that go out on the lake.
25 It was amazing. They also have really great pizza and hot
26 dogs in Chicago. Yeah, Chicago is ... well, I highly
27 recommend it. My dream vacation? That's easy. Paris. I
28 would love to go to Paris. For some reason, my parents have

1   always hesitated to take my sister and I to Europe. I think
2   they might be saving it for a graduation present or
3   something like that. But, anyway, I'm dying to go. I take
4   French in school, so it would be really special for me. Have
5   you been? If so, I'm really, really jealous. Maybe if we
6   become really good friends, we could go there together one
7   day. *(Smiles.)* Or not. Time will only tell, right? *(Sighs.)* So,
8   the next thing you wanted to know about is what I want to
9   be. That's easy. I want to be a pediatrician. I love kids and
10 would like to be able to help them. Especially
11 underprivileged children, you know. I think that would be so
12 rewarding. Plus, they make a lot of money, too. Which
13 doesn't hurt. I mean, I do realize that my parents won't
14 always be there to provide for me or want to provide for me
15 for that matter. I mean, they'll expect me to get out on my
16 own. So yeah, I think me being a doctor would make them
17 proud. My hero? That's my dad. Hands down. I hope you'll
18 meet him one day. He's ... the best. My ideal guy? Well, he's
19 kind, considerate, and fun to be with, of course. And I'm
20 hoping ... you're the one. Is it you?

44. Spoiled Rotten

1   I admit it; I'm spoiled rotten. I truly am. And I guess I
2 have been since ... well, I can remember. But I ask you, is
3 that my fault? Am I to blame? Absolutely not. I never asked
4 to be spoiled. It's something that my parents, my
5 grandparents, my aunts, and my uncles have done to me.
6 So if I'm rude, ungrateful, and lazy, I have only them to
7 blame. Really, did I have to go to the Ritz in Paris for my
8 thirteenth birthday? According to my grandmother I did. Did
9 I have to have a pony when I was five? Daddy thought so.
10 When we went to an amusement park, did I have to be the
11 first to get on every ride with the five-hundred-dollar
12 Princess of the Day pass? Probably not. But that's just the
13 way things have always been. In a way it makes me angry.
14 I mean, what did I need more? To have the world handed to
15 me on a silver platter or a little discipline and some self
16 respect? The way I see it is that I've been ruined. Absolutely
17 nothing pleases me anymore. I look at things and well, I'm
18 completely bored. New dresses? Bored. A new car? Bored.
19 A ski trip with Poppy? Bored. It's all completely boring to
20 me. The one thing I do want is ... well, I should say the one
21 person I do want is Brandon Sommers. And Brandon? He'll
22 have nothing to do with me. Because I'm spoiled rotten, you
23 see. Sad, isn't it?

45. Just Shooting the Breeze

1   So ... what do you think of Marjory? Marjory is a cute
2   name for a cat. *(Rolling her eyes)* OK. So you don't like
3   Marjory. What about Sam? It's short for Samantha, dummy,
4   so it's actually a perfect name for a girl cat. OK. So, you
5   don't like Sam either. I know! You're gonna love this one!
6   What about Cupcake? You don't like Cupcake either. OK. So
7   you've given the thumbs down to Marjory, Sam, and
8   Cupcake. Do you mind if I ask, "What name do you like for
9   our new cat?" And don't say you just want to name it Cat.
10   Why not? Because, nitwit, we already have a cat named
11   Dog, so that would be totally lame. Besides, if we did that,
12   I think we would give Dog a complex. Yes, we would. He
13   would be like, *(Imitating boy's voice)* "Why did they name me
14   Dog and give her a nice name like Cat. What's wrong with
15   me? Do I bark in my sleep or something?" So no, ixnay on
16   the name atcay. *(Rolling her eyes)* I'm talking Pig Latin,
17   Stupid, because Dog just walked in the room and I don't
18   even want him to know that you even suggested calling the
19   new girl cat ... you know ... *that.* I mean, I couldn't even
20   believe that Mom let you call Dog *Dog* in the first place. Poor
21   thing. That's probably why he always walks around with that
22   sour look on his face and tries to scratch you when you try
23   to pet him. Yeah, that is too why. I'll bet you a million
24   dollars. Poor thing's been traumatized. OK, so anyway, what
25   other lame ideas do you have? *(Listens then puts finger in her*
26   *mouth like she's going to throw up.)* That is even worse than
27   Cat. These are your ideas and you didn't like Cupcake?
28   There is something seriously wrong with you. I think you've

1   been eating too many potato chips and the salt has made
2   your brain retain water. Hey, by the way, are there any left?
3   Two?! Two?! What a hog. You've eaten the whole thing. Give
4   me the two that are left. I'm starving. What do you mean one
5   for me and one for you? That's ridiculous. You've already
6   eaten about a hundred. No way. Come on, give them to me.
7   *(Holds out her hand, then smiles.)* **Thank you very much!**
8   *(Eating the chips)* **Hey, look over there. Across the street.**
9   Looks like Lisa Peabody has another boyfriend. Nice car, eh?
10 Oh, geez, no, that's some old guy. Lisa wouldn't be caught
11 dead with him. He must be for her mother. Yeah, her mother
12 dates all the time. Duh, the Peabodys got divorced two years
13 ago, space case. Yes, they did. Just watch, Ms. Peabody's
14 gonna come out all dolled up with about five inches of
15 makeup on her face and that crazy blue eye shadow.
16 Somebody needs to tell her that just makes her look insane.
17 I'm not gonna tell her. Why don't you? Anyway, she must be
18 doing something right. At least she gets dates. Unlike Mom
19 who hasn't had a date in about a hundred years. Of course
20 I want Mom to date. Don't you? How else are we ever gonna
21 get a father figure? Yeah, I know you don't want one 'cause
22 you want to be the "man of the house". But, I do want one.
23 And Mom does, too. I mean, she doesn't want a father
24 figure, she wants a husband. Yes, she does. I don't care if
25 she says it or not. Believe me, every woman wants one.
26 What do you mean, how do I know? I'm a girl, aren't I? Plus,
27 I read. Magazines, the Internet. You know. Women's stuff.
28 And, there are only about fifty thousand articles a day on
29 how to get one. A husband, dummy. Yes, it is true. You
30 know, it wouldn't hurt you to read some of those articles.
31 You being a boy and all that. Well, you know, you could get
32 the female perspective. Well, you may not care now, but you
33 will one day. One day, you're gonna go out with some chick
34 for a while and if you don't pop the question, she's gonna
35 pop you. She will if she has any sense, anyway. Geez, you

1 really don't have a clue. *(Looks across the street again.)* **Oh,**
2 **look. Ms. Peabody and Mr. Wonderful are coming out the**
3 **door.** *(Laughing)* **See, what did I tell you? Blue eye shadow!**
4 *(Laughing harder)* **You can see it all the way across the**
5 **street.** *(Stops laughing.)* **Hey, maybe I ought to tell Mom to**
6 **get some. No, seriously. Maybe that's the ticket. You know,**
7 **to catching a man.** *(Thinking about it seriously)* **Hmmmm.**
8 **Lots of blue eye shadow. You know I don't think it would**
9 **hurt if Mom flirted a little either. She's so serious, you**
10 **know. I've seen her talking to guys! Of course I have. She**
11 **talks to the mailman, the butcher, our orthodontist. I don't**
12 **know if they're married or not, but she could still flirt a little,**
13 **you know. At least for practice. I don't know if she even**
14 **knows how. Probably not.** *(Mumbles.)* **I don't know.** *(Louder)*
15 **I don't know! How would I know if she flirted with our dad.**
16 **Why did you even have to bring him up? You know I don't**
17 **like to talk about that. Him. Whatever.** *(Quiets for a moment.*
18 *Thinks.)* **Let's change the subject. What are we gonna name**
19 **the cat? I know! Shadow! Yeah, Shadow, like as in "blue eye**
20 **shadow". You like it? You really do? OK, pinch me, I must**
21 **be dreaming — you actually like my idea. Amazing! OK, that**
22 **settles it, then. So now we have Dog and Shadow. How cool**
23 **is that?**

46. Wedding Bells

1   Hey, Blake! Guess what? Some big news. See if you can
2   guess. A hint? OK, let's see. How about ... *(Hums the*
3   *wedding march as she pretends to be a bride walking down the*
4   *aisle.)* **Dum, dum, da, dum. Dum, dum, da, dum. No! I'm not**
5   **getting married. But somebody is!** *(Squeals with delight.)* **My**
6   **parents! Can you believe it! Yes, yes, yes, yes.** *(Dances*
7   *around with happiness.)* **This is going to be soooo great. They**
8   **just told me this morning and I've been, like, walking on air**
9   **ever since. Yes, yes, yes. Can you believe it? I mean they've**
10   **always told me it didn't matter, but it always mattered to**
11   **me. And now my dream is coming true. Saturday! They're**
12   **doing it this Saturday! Will you come? I'm going to be a**
13   **bridesmaid! Crazy, right? A bridesmaid at my mom and**
14   **dad's wedding. I cannot wait. We're going shopping**
15   **tomorrow for dresses. Mom, of course, is going to wear**
16   **white and she says I can pick any color I want. Oh, get this!**
17   **My brother Tim is going to be the best man! He's going to**
18   **wear a tux! No, he'll have to rent one. It's going to be in our**
19   **backyard or at the beach. They haven't decided yet. I'm**
20   **begging them to do the beach. The backyard just seems**
21   **kind of lame. I think it would be so cool if they got married**
22   **at sunrise. Sunrise on the beach? Super romantic, right?**
23   **Hmmmm? Oh, I don't know. I really don't know what finally**
24   **made them decide to do it. I was so excited I didn't even**
25   **ask. Maybe they were hungry for wedding cake?** *(Laughs.)*
26   **Oh, Blake, I think this is the best day of my life.**

47. The Breakup — Tara's Story

1   It's over. Alonzo and I broke up. What do you mean,
2   "Why aren't I crying?" Why should I cry? There are other fish
3   in the sea. It's not a big deal. Really. In fact, I kind of like
4   someone else already. Who broke up with who? What do you
5   think? Of course I broke up with him. He's been getting on
6   my nerves for a long time. And he was kind of boring, too,
7   you know. Never wanted to do anything fun. Always wanted
8   to bring his friends with us everywhere. Very immature. You
9   know? My mother told me that girls mature faster than
10   guys, but I didn't believe her. Until now, that is. Hmmmm?
11   How long were we going out? About a year. Yeah, that's a
12   long time. Seemed even longer sometimes 'cause I was so
13   bored. I don't know. I really don't know why I didn't do it
14   sooner. Just lazy I guess. Well, and I guess I didn't want to
15   hurt Alonzo's feelings either. I do have a heart, you know.
16   And you know it won't be easy for him to get another girl.
17   Oh, well. I couldn't stay with him forever just out of
18   sympathy. Only a fool would do that. It will take time, but
19   he'll get over it. I'm sure. But that's not my problem
20   anymore. My problem is who am I gonna go out with
21   Saturday night? I think Bennie is gonna ask me, but he's so
22   shy he may not be able to get up the nerve. Bennie? You
23   know, that new kid in second period. Yeah, that's the guy
24   I've got my eye on. I can tell he likes me, but he probably
25   heard that I was going with Alonzo so he thought he didn't
26   have a chance. Now word will get out and it won't be long
27   'til he makes his move. That's why I'm glad Alonzo and I are
28   over for good. It was just time. You know? Time to move on.

48. They Love Me, I Love Them Not

1   Being popular at school has done me no good at all. It's
2 true! Well, for example, there are about five guys at school
3 who really like me a lot. Unfortunately, not one of them is
4 the guy I want. What's wrong with them? Well, let's see ...
5 where do I begin? T.J. is real cute but he has a whiny voice.
6 No, not just a whiny voice, but *(Imitating him)* a super whiny
7 voice. Don't get me wrong, he's really, really cute, but when
8 he talks? Forget about it. And Brad? He doesn't have a
9 whiny voice, but I hardly know what kind of voice he has at
10 all. 'Cause, most of the time he never says a word. It totally
11 spooks me out. I mean, who knows what he's thinking. Or
12 if he's thinking. Right? Maybe he's not thinking at all?
13 Maybe he's like from the land of the zombies. OK, so then
14 there's Ricky. From a distance I really, really like Ricky a lot.
15 But up close? I'm totally allergic to him. Seriously. I don't
16 know if he has cats or dogs or a mule, but whatever he has
17 he wears their hair on his clothes all the time and I just
18 don't have the heart to tell him. But I'll be walking down the
19 hall at school and my nose starts to itch and my eyes start
20 to water and I'll look around and, sure enough, there he is.
21 So when I see Ricky, I run. The other way, that is. And let's
22 see, what other guy has a crush on me? I've named
23 *(Counting on her fingers)* T.J., Brad, Ricky. Did I mention
24 Tony? Oh, OK. Tony. Tony is a doll. He really is. He's cute.
25 Nice voice. No animals. But his parents own an Italian
26 restaurant and his breath? Garlic morning noon and night. I
27 love garlic as much as anybody else, but for breakfast? Get
28 real! So let's see who else. Ah, yes, last but not least ...

1 Ivan. Ivan is someone that could really drive you up a wall.
2 He's cute, nice voice, no animals, and no garlic, but he is
3 the biggest know-it-all you have ever met in your life! OMG!
4 If you think you know the answer, Ivan always has a better
5 one. It's like an hour or two around Ivan and I want to just
6 explode. I know he's just trying to impress me, but come
7 on. Does he have to always be right? So you see how it is.
8 Being popular has gotten me nowhere at all, at least in the
9 department of romance. I've got five guys that totally adore
10 me and not one of them is right. And the one that I want?
11 Doesn't seem to know I'm alive. Who? Oh, the guy that I
12 love is just perfect. Larry. What's so great about Larry?
13 Well, like I said, Larry is perfect. Cute as a button, a voice
14 as smooth as glass, never had an animal in his life, he's
15 allergic to garlic, and best of all? I don't ever have to worry
16 about him being a know-it-all like Ivan. No, not a chance.
17 Larry? He's as dumb as a stump.

49. Is It My Turn Yet?

1   **Mom! Mom! Guess what! Look! Look what I got.** *(Waves*
2   *a piece of paper in the air then sees her mom enter in a beautiful*
3   *evening gown.)* **Wow! Where are you going?**
4   **You look soooo beautiful!** *(Puts paper down on the dining*
5   *room table.)* **Sure, let me help.** *(Helping her mom hook up the*
6   *dress)* **Mom, this dress! It's amazing! When did you get it?**
7   **Today? You left work early? Oh, he needs you to attend an**
8   **event tonight! Wow! Your boss is so lucky to have you. Look**
9   **at you! You look like … a million dollars. Take your picture?**
10 **Sure.** *(Takes her phone out of her purse.)* **Here, I'll use my**
11 **phone. Smile! Oh, hey, I'm getting a call.** *(Looks at the*
12 *number.)* **It's Grandma. Oh, OK, Mom, have a good time.**
13 **You look great. Hi, Grandma, Guess what I got today?**
14 **Grandma? Grandma, are you crying? You did what? You fell?**
15 **That's terrible! Are you OK? Should I call an ambulance?**
16 **Oh, thank goodness. It just gave you a good scare, then?**
17 **Oh, no, you hurt your ankle? Yeah, sure, sure, I can pick up**
18 **your prescriptions for you. The drug store on the corner by**
19 **your house? Sure, Gram, I'll get them right away. Do you**
20 **need me to take you to Urgent Care for your ankle? OK. OK.**
21 **One of those things with ice? Oh, yeah, like an ice pack.**
22 **Yeah, sure, Gram, I'll pick one of those up, too. You've got**
23 **some ice on it now though, right? That's good. And you**
24 **should elevate it, too.** *(Louder)* **I said you should elevate it.**
25 *You should put your foot up!* **Oh, OK, good. Gram, I'm**
26 **worried about you. Will you be all right 'til I get there? OK.**
27 **OK. I'll see you soon.** *(Looks at her watch.)* **I've just got to**
28 **feed the cats before I go. Real fast. But then I'm on my way.**

1   **OK, Gram. I love you.** *(Hangs up the phone, exhales, and then*
2   *goes to the cupboard for the cat food.)* **Let's see ... where is the**
3   **cat food. Aha!** *(Opens the can and sees the cat at her feet.)* **Hey,**
4   **Fluffy! How was your day?** *(Feeding the cat)* **I got some good**
5   **news today. It's over there on the table. Why don't you read**
6   **it while I'm gone and we'll talk about it when I get back.**
7   **That is, if you've got the time.**

50. Shy

1   I hate it when everyone always says, "You're so shy" or
2 "You're so quiet." It just makes me feel more shy and
3 makes me more quiet. I wish they'd just ignore me and let
4 me be me. Then maybe I'd, you know, come out of my shell
5 a little bit. I don't know. I guess I'm quiet because I don't
6 know what to say most of the time. Maybe that's why I like
7 acting. Somebody else thinks up the words and the feelings
8 and you just have to memorize them and act them out.
9 Then I'm not shy at all. Funny, isn't it? I'm more
10 comfortable being someone else than being me. I don't
11 know, I don't think it's so bad to be shy. Or quiet, for that
12 matter. Sometimes I think it's the quiet people who notice
13 things. You know? Like ... well, like at the Open House Band
14 Concert last year, I was sitting beside Freddy McGuire. And
15 Todd Bright was sitting on the other side of him. We were all
16 swarming around and the kids were all talking or starting to
17 warm up. That's when Ms. Burly comes over to Freddy and
18 asks him why he isn't wearing a black T-shirt. See, the
19 dress code for the concert was black pants and a black
20 T-shirt. Freddy mumbled that his mother had said she
21 would bring him one, but hadn't gotten there yet. Ms. Burly
22 says, "If she's not here in five minutes, you're not in the
23 concert tonight." She walked away and I saw Freddy's eyes
24 start to fill with tears. He knew his mother wouldn't come.
25 He started to pack up and then he left. And everyone else?
26 They never even noticed. I wrote a short story about it in
27 English class this year. Of course I changed the names to
28 protect the innocent. My English teacher, Mr. Freidman, had

1 me read my story to the class out loud. Todd Bright, the guy
2 who was sitting on the other side of Freddy at the Open
3 House Band Concert, came up to me after class and said,
4 "That story was awesome! Did you just make that up, or
5 did something like that really happen to you." See, what did
6 I tell you? It's the quiet people like me who notice things
7 while most of the world goes around ... well, oblivious. I
8 don't think I'm a great person though or anything. I mean,
9 just for noticing stuff. To me, a really great person is
10 someone who notices stuff and does something about it to
11 make things better. My grandmother Myrtle is that kind of
12 person. She notices when people are down or lonely or sick
13 and she does something right away, something personal, to
14 make it better. Even if it's just to give them a smile and say
15 hello. I wish I could be more like that. Like at the Open
16 House Band Concert last year. I wish I had just gotten up
17 and told Freddy that he could have my T-shirt. I could have
18 gone to the dressing room, gotten in my school clothes, and
19 told my parents that I couldn't play that night. You know,
20 something like, "I just came out of the bathroom where I
21 threw up and had to throw away my black T-shirt, it was so
22 gross." I just never think of stuff like that until about a year
23 later. Like now. Freddy didn't take band class this year, so
24 I guess he just didn't want to face it all again. The
25 disappointment, the humiliation. I can understand that. But
26 it makes me sad. I saw him in the hall the other day and I
27 wanted to go up and say hello, but I didn't. I was, you know,
28 just too shy.

Monologues
for Guys

1. What I Did This Summer

1   It's so predictable. Every school year, at the start of the
2   year, some teacher, most likely in English, will give us that
3   age-old assignment to write about "What I did on summer
4   vacation." I find this assignment particularly painful and
5   although I dutifully do the assignment, I almost never tell
6   the truth. How can I? Well, for instance, how will the
7   eggheads in my class understand what I mean when I say
8   that I spent much of the summer reading Brecht? Or that I
9   totally came to understand the philosophy of Hegel? Will
10   they even know who Brecht and Hegel are? Of course not.
11   You see, I'm a square peg. A kid who doesn't fit in and who
12   never will. Mind you, not fitting in is fine with me. However,
13   I do what I can to make it a little less noticeable if and when
14   possible. And by that I mean, I don't tell anyone what I did
15   for summer vacation. Not this summer or last summer, or
16   ever. No, I simply make something up. I tell them I went to
17   visit my aunt in Colorado where we went hiking and biking
18   almost every day. I say that I loved staying up all hours
19   watching reruns of some ridiculous television sitcom that
20   I've actually never seen. I make up some emergency that
21   happened to which I had to heroically react, such as my
22   cousin Toby fell out of a tree and I had to run fifteen miles
23   to get to the nearest house to get help because neither of
24   us had our cell phones with us that day. It's rather fun
25   making this stuff up and I do so prefer it to letting anyone
26   know just exactly how different I am. But still, I'd rather not
27   do the assignment at all. It does make one long for the days
28   when childhood and adolescence will be left behind and as

1   a grown man, if asked, "What did you do this summer?" I
2   can just simply say, "With all due respect, mind your own
3   beeswax."

2. Are You for Real?

1   I can't remember what it's like to not be lonely. It's like
2   a few years back, it just became one of the defining
3   characteristics of who I am — the lonely guy. It doesn't
4   matter if I'm in a crowd of people. I just can't ever seem to
5   connect. Why? I don't know. If I knew the answer to that, I
6   wouldn't be so lonely, I guess. I don't know. I can't really
7   remember the last time I really had fun either. Or the last
8   time I really laughed. Sure, I can chuckle along with
9   everyone else when something stupid happens in class or
10   when something happens in a movie that's supposed to be
11   funny. Maybe I'm depressed. Nothing makes me happy. Or
12   maybe I'm not depressed, I'm just really, really unhappy for
13   a really, really good reason. Well, that is, actually many,
14   many good reasons. What does it mean to be depressed,
15   anyway? All the ads on TV make it seem like depression is,
16   well, it's all about how you just aren't able to enjoy the good
17   life anymore. But, I mean, what if there isn't any good life
18   anymore? At least not for you, anyway. What if all the good
19   stuff you used to enjoy was just an illusion and now you can
20   see life as it really is and it just totally sucks? What are you
21   supposed to do about that? Take some magic pill that
22   makes you think everything is just peachy again when it
23   never really was in the first place? I don't know. Maybe I
24   should be a philosopher. I am having really deep thoughts.
25   Like, is anything real at all? Are you for real? When I see you
26   walk up to me at school with a smile on your face, are you
27   really happy? When I hear you laugh at some dumb joke or
28   something stupid on TV, are you really laughing? Seriously.

1 Are you really laughing at something funny or are you just
2 pretending to laugh because you think that's what is
3 expected of you in certain situations? Do you ever really say
4 what you mean? See, I feel like this, we are all born as our
5 real selves and then as we grow up we learn to hide
6 everything that's real and true. We learn to fit in and we
7 learn to please. Yeah. We learn to totally please our parents.
8 To please our teachers. Please our friends. And then, one
9 day, like a bolt of lightning out of the blue, some of us just
10 wake up and we're suddenly tired of pleasing. It doesn't
11 make us happy anymore. But by then we can't even
12 remember who we really were. Before we started pleasing
13 everybody. So all we can do is walk around this planet like
14 a zombie. Like we're in a dream. And when we look in the
15 mirror, all we can say is, "Who am I, anyway?" "Who was it
16 that I used to be?" "Am I for real?" "Are you for real?" Wow.
17 It's crazy isn't it? You see what I mean, right?

3. The Banana Splits

1   I'm getting tired of this gig. Here it is, another Saturday
2   morning and I'm spending it with you at another little kid's
3   birthday party. Yeah, yeah, I know, we're making money, but
4   still ... no offense, I mean, this was a great idea your mom
5   had, putting us together in a little kids' band, you know, us
6   dressing up like fruit and calling ourselves the Fruity
7   Tooties. But, you know, I'm not sure I'm having so much fun
8   with this anymore. And how come I have to be the banana?
9   I said from the beginning that I'd rather be the orange, but
10   nobody listened to me. I did, too. David you remember me
11   saying that, right? Yeah, I did! What is this? Doesn't
12   anybody remember? Well, anyway, who cares. If I'm the
13   banana or if I'm a doggone prune, I am tired of being in this
14   band. If we're gonna keep working together we need to start
15   working on music that we like. Or maybe nobody
16   remembers that we used to like the same music, either?
17   These kiddy tunes are driving me nuts. Yeah, yeah, I know
18   we said it was only for a little while, but face it guys we
19   never get together to play anything for real anymore. All of
20   our spare time is spent on this junk. Yeah, yeah, I've heard
21   that before. "After this party we'll get serious." After this
22   party there will be another party and another party, and hey,
23   I'm not doing it anymore. *(Starts taking off his banana*
24   *costume.)* What does it look like I'm doing? I'm peeling off
25   this banana costume and getting the heck out of here. You'll
26   be fine. You don't need a banana. And if you do, you can find
27   some other tall skinny guy who likes to wear fruit, 'cause
28   this banana ... is gonna split.

4. Who Am I?

1   Sometimes I just wish I was anybody but me. You know
2   what I mean? Naw, how could you. Your life is great. Yes, it
3   is. You have a mom and a dad. OK, stepdad. Whatever. You
4   live in a house with two dogs. Your life is awesome. I live
5   with my grandma in a trailer and I don't even have a
6   goldfish. *(Sighs.)* Naw, it's not that. I love my grandma. I
7   actually like our trailer, too. It's not that at all. It's me. It's
8   who I am. What? Who is that? Very funny. Sam Waters, idiot.
9   What do you mean who am I really? I'm fifteen years old. I'm
10   not smart. Who says I'm not smart? Are you kidding?
11   Everybody. Who's everybody? Geez, what's with you today?
12   Well, you're asking a lot of questions. OK. Who is
13   everybody? OK, well, maybe nobody said it in exactly those
14   words. Like, Mrs. Frasier for instance. She never said,
15   "Sam, you're not smart." But, it's the way she treats me in
16   class. The way she rolls her eyes at things I say. Everybody
17   knows it. All the kids in class. You could ask any of them.
18   She thinks I'm not smart and so do they. They may not say
19   it, but it's true. And hey, I'm not even arguing with them.
20   It's like I said, sometimes, I just wish I was anybody but
21   me. OK, OK, maybe not anybody. Yeah, yeah, lots of other
22   people are dumber than I am. OK, so, I said the wrong
23   thing. I wish I was somebody smarter than me. What else?
24   What else do I wish was different about me? Well, OK, if you
25   must know, I wish I was better looking. No, not like a movie
26   star. Like a superstar athlete with all the girls. That kind of
27   look. That's what I wish I had. Naw, I'm scrawny. I'm
28   scrawny. You know, I have no muscles. I'm weak. Yeah, so

1   what if I am only fifteen. Lots of guys at school my age are
2   strong. Yeah, I could exercise. I could, but I don't think it
3   would do any good. Well, yeah, I did try last summer for a
4   while. I did push-ups. For my arms and my chest. I didn't
5   see any difference. How many? I don't know. Maybe fifty.
6   Aw, I don't know, I stopped after about a week. I was tired.
7   It was hot last summer. Our air conditioner broke and all I
8   wanted to do was lay around. *(Sighs.)* OK, well, there you go,
9   I'm lazy. So that's another thing I don't like about myself.
10 I'm lazy. I wish I was the kind of guy who got things done.
11 You know, like Clark. Yeah, like Clark. That guy is always
12 working on something and whatever he's working on always
13 works out. Me, I'm lazy. But you know what? Even if I wasn't
14 lazy, nothing would work out for me anyway. I know. I do
15 know. How do I know? Well, 'cause there have been times in
16 my life when I wasn't lazy and nothing worked out. That's
17 how I know. An example? *(Sighs.)* Man, you're making me
18 tired. Yeah, I'm getting tired. That's another thing! I wish I
19 had more energy. Yeah. More energy. Maybe if I had more
20 energy I wouldn't be so lazy. And then maybe once in a
21 while something I did would work out. You know. I mean, I'd
22 like to have so much energy that I just kept trying and then
23 eventually something would work out. What do you mean
24 that takes more than energy? A positive attitude? Yeah,
25 that's another thing I wish I had. A positive attitude. I know
26 my attitude sucks. You can't just make yourself have a
27 positive attitude. No, you can't. That's ... I don't think that's
28 true. So you're saying I'm supposed to wake up in the
29 morning and check my attitude and if it ain't positive I'm
30 supposed to just turn it around. *(Sighs.)* I don't know. I just
31 don't know. That sounds like something I wish I could do,
32 but that would never work for me. I told you! Stuff I do just
33 doesn't work out. And I'm too tired when I wake up in the
34 morning to sit there and work on my attitude. Yeah, I'm tired
35 when I wake up. Aren't you? Well, you're just perfect, man.

1   You are. It's like I said, your life is great. You have a mom
2   and a dad. *OK, a stepdad!* Geez, *whatever.* And you live in a
3   house with two dogs. You have a positive attitude, lots of
4   energy, and you never wake up tired. You're great, Ricky.
5   You're just great. You are just great. In fact, you're so great
6   it's disgusting. You know what? I would rather be me than
7   you. Yeah, I would. In fact, I like me. I like being tired. I like
8   being lazy. And now that I think about it, I even like being
9   scrawny. I'm not so bad looking either. And I *am* smart. I
10 don't care what Mrs. Frasier says or what she or those idiots
11 in class think about me. At least I know who I am. Yeah, I
12 do. I know exactly who I am. And that's good enough for me.

5. Lunchroom Bully

1   *(Nick walks up to Harold at the cafeteria table.)* **Hey Harold,**
2   **you gonna eat your cake? Oh, yeah? How about if I stick my**
3   **finger in it like this?** *(Licks his finger.)* **You still gonna eat it?**
4   *(Picks up the cake and shoves it in his mouth. With mouth full)*
5   **Yeah, I didn't think you were gonna eat it. Wouldn't want it**
6   **to go to waste. Mind if I join you?** *(Sits down.)* **So Harold,**
7   **that's a pretty nice car you drove up to school in today. Is**
8   **it yours? Really? Wow. Must be nice. A new sports car for**
9   **your sixteenth birthday. So how come you're in here eating**
10   **lunch with these bums. You could be out having lunch at the**
11   **Burger Shack with me. You're eatin' fast so you can study**
12   **afterwards? You study at lunch, Harold? OK, OK, I can dig**
13   **that. I guess that's why you're such a brain. But Harold, you**
14   **got to take me to the Burger Shack tomorrow, OK? Are you**
15   **OK with that? Yeah, I thought you would be. How many fit**
16   **in that car of yours? Just two? OK, you can cram somebody**
17   **in the back. OK, well that's good. You see that guy over**
18   **there with all the tattoos? That's Sid. He's gonna come too,**
19   **OK? Yeah, he can squeeze in the back. You just said that**
20   **somebody can squeeze in the back. Oh, yeah? He's too big?**
21   *(Looks over at Sid.)* **Yeah, I guess he's kind of a big guy. Yeah,**
22   **I can see that might be true. Well, that's too bad, see,**
23   **'cause Sid and I need to get to the Burger Shack tomorrow**
24   **and your car only seats two. Hey! Hey! I just got a brilliant**
25   **idea. You know, like in the cartoons when a light bulb goes**
26   **on inside some guy's head. Yeah. Sid and I can just borrow**
27   **your car tomorrow and you can stay here with these bums**
28   **and then go study. Yeah, that's what we'll do. You don't**

1   know? Whaddya mean you don't know? *(Looking very angry)*
2   Harold, aren't we friends? I mean, don't you want to be my
3   friend? Of course you do. Of course you do, Harold. Yeah, I
4   know you worry about the car and all that but, Harold, you
5   ain't got nothin' to worry about. See, I'm a good driver and
6   so is Sid. We'll take good care of your baby, see. Yeah, real
7   good care. And we'll have her back before the end of the
8   school day so that you can get home to your mother and
9   she'll never know a thing. Harold, we are just going to the
10 Burger Shack but afterwards I might need to run an errand
11 for my sick grandma, you know. Like pick up her medicine
12 or something. You know, some kind of emergency like that.
13 Are you sayin' you'd want my grandma to go without her
14 medicine? If she has some kind of attack she could die.
15 Yeah, we'll get it back before the end of the school day,
16 Harold. *(Looks over at Sid.)* I've gotta split, Harold, but it was
17 real nice talkin' to you. I'll meet you here tomorrow same
18 time and get the keys, OK? OK, Harold? Yeah, OK. Maybe
19 if they have the cake tomorrow you'll get the chocolate one,
20 alright? That white cake is kinda stale all the time, you
21 know. And since you're not gonna eat it, anyway. Thank
22 you, Harold. You're a good friend, you know that. Tomorrow,
23 man. Tomorrow same time. Don't let me down now. I don't
24 like it when a friend lets me down. It hurts me right here.
25 *(Holds his heart.)* And then I can't help it, I just go crazy. Like
26 I could kill somebody or somethin'. *(Sighs.)* Yeah, I gotta
27 work on my temper. That's what my ma says. OK, Harold,
28 I'll see you tomorrow. You're a real pal.

6. Something Stinks in Here!

1   Oh, holy tomatoes! Something royally stinks in here!
2 Geez, Broderick, do you ever clean your bedroom? It smells
3 like dirty socks and old hamburgers. With onions. Do you
4 have a clothespin I can put on my nose? Dude, I can't leave,
5 I came to get my stuff. Yeah, my stuff. All the stuff you've
6 borrowed from me over the last two years. You know we're
7 moving today and you said you'd have everything ready for
8 me. You forgot? How could you forget? Dude, I need my
9 stuff. Where is it? Broderick, come clean. Do you have my
10 stuff or not? You're not sure. Not sure? What does that
11 mean? You might have accidentally sold it? What do you
12 mean accidentally? Your parents' garage sale? Last week?
13 Last week? Dude, at least you could have let me know it
14 was for sale so I could have bought my own stuff back.
15 Dude, you're too much. Something really does stink in here.
16 And it's not just your socks.

7. Shooting Hoops

1   Tom and I, we practice every day. Same gym, same
2   time, but for totally different reasons. See, for Tom, it's just
3   shooting hoops. To me, it's my life. It really is my life. Not
4   just now, like as in, "All I think about is basketball," but as
5   in my future. Without basketball I've got no future. It's my
6   only chance of getting a scholarship to college. Tom, he's
7   got rich parents. He's got college all sewed up. So you see,
8   when we're shooting hoops, it's different for me than it is for
9   Tom. *(Starts dribbling a ball.)* I have a lot of hopes and
10 dreams. *(Shoots.)* I want to go to college. *(Gets ball again and
11 shoots.)* I want to be a doctor. *(Shoots again.)* Oh, man, how
12 did I miss that? Dang. See, I can't make mistakes like that.
13 I can't. It's too important. I want to help my mother. I want
14 to help my brothers and sisters. I want to help my
15 granddaddy and grandma. You understand now, right? See,
16 Tom's thinking about how cool he'll look at the game. I'm
17 thinking I've got to do great things with the game. I've got
18 to be great. If I'm not, I'm letting a lot of people down. My
19 family, you know. My mother. My mother has sacrificed
20 everything for us kids. She's worked three jobs for a long,
21 long time. I've got to be a role model, too, for my brothers
22 and sisters. My brothers and sisters look up to me. I can't
23 let them down. I just can't. If I don't get to college, I'll ... I'll
24 never forgive myself. So you see, for me, it's not about
25 shooting hoops. It's about shooting for my dreams.

8. Radical Road Trip

1   Last year my friends and I took a radical road trip. It was
2   like, radish, man. No, not like a radish. *(Laughs a funny*
3   *laugh that sounds a little more like a snort.)* Naw, not like the
4   vegetable, dude. I mean it was radish, like in totally radical.
5   *(Laughs again.)* You're such a freak. So anyway, this road
6   trip was like, amazing. Big Jim got his driver's license and
7   his parents bought him a new car. Yeah, dude. They think
8   he's "responsible." He's totally out of his mind though so we
9   had an awesome time. Yeah, we went everywhere but our
10   main destination was the Grand Canyon. Dude, have you
11   been there? Aw, man, you have got to go. It's totally radical,
12   dude. Righteously radical. We were like, so stoked just
13   looking at it. Big Jim kept acting like he was gonna fall off
14   the edge though which was kind of annoying. I mean, that
15   happens for real there all the time. Yeah, man, I read some
16   lady was taking her daughter's picture and her daughter
17   took one step back and it was like woooo down into never,
18   never land. Yeah, man. It totally sucked. Yeah, but we saw
19   a bunch of stuff, dude. We drove down the strip in Vegas.
20   Crazy, man. Crazy. I'm going back when I'm twenty-one for
21   sure. Then we drove on to California. Dude, you should have
22   seen the waves. We didn't have boards but there were some
23   righteous dudes that let us catch some waves on theirs. It
24   was totally radical. Man, I think that was the best summer
25   of my life. Seriously, dude. I mean my whole life. I know that
26   will never happen again. It was like everything just fell into
27   place. Summer vacation, Big Jim's new car, and my parents
28   taking a total mental vacation and letting me go for some
29   weird reason. It's like some things are just meant to be.

9. Farewell Goofy-Foot

1   *(Looking out the window)* **So Goofy-Foot is really leaving.**
2   Yep. The moving truck just pulled up. Naw, I'm not goin'
3   over to say good-bye. What for? All my friends end up
4   leaving and I'm not saying good-bye anymore. But I sure am
5   gonna miss old Goofy-Foot. We had some awesome times
6   together, him and I. You know when he first moved in I
7   didn't think we'd be friends at all. He just looked weird, you
8   know. He still looks weird, but in a good way. There's just
9   nobody else like Goofy-Foot. I still remember the first time
10   we went up Rattler's Hill together. He was so awesome,
11   man. I'm afraid of heights but he just kept on goin' ahead
12   of me. I had a hard time keeping up but he gave me the
13   courage, you know. It's just not gonna be the same goin' up
14   that hill without Goofy-Foot charging ahead of me. And
15   remember the time we all got takeout from Sloppy Poppy's
16   Rib Shack? I swear I never saw anybody tear into ribs the
17   way Goofy-Foot did. He acted like he never had ribs in his
18   life before. Yeah, Goofy-Foot just made everything seem so
19   outrageously better than it was before I met him. And of
20   course I'll never ever forget the first time I saw him on a
21   board. What he did on that board was totally sick. Yep, I
22   sure am gonna miss that dawg.

10. Rattlesnake!

1   *(Taking the last few steps to the top of the mountain)* **Oh ...**
2 **man! This is it! This is it! The top of the mountain! Man, the**
3 **world is so ... beautiful from up here.** *(Yells.)* **Woo hoo!** *(Fists*
4 *high in the air, yells again.)* **We're here!** *(Listens to the echo and*
5 *shouts while beating on his chest.)* **We made it!** *(Listens to the*
6 *echo. Then says to his friend)* **We've conquered the mountain.**
7 *(Looking at his friend)* **Can you believe it? I can't believe it. I**
8 **can't even believe it, man. I mean, I've been working up to**
9 **this for a year. Look at me. Me! The kid who used to be**
10 **afraid of heights. Now look at me.** *(Jumping around)* **I'm on**
11 **the top of the mountain.** *(Laughing)* **I could fall off at any**
12 **moment and there is no fear.** *(Shouting)* **You hear me world?**
13 *No fear! (To his friend)* **It's like I'm a new person up here.**
14 **Totally, I mean totally without fear. It's true. Man, I am so**
15 **fearless up here that I can walk right to the edge, like this.**
16 *(Walks over.)* **Did you ever think you'd see me do this? See.**
17 *(Dangles one foot off the edge.)* **No fear. Did you ever think**
18 **you'd see me do this?** *(Does something such as a hip hop*
19 *dance move, cartwheel, etc.)* **How about this?** *(Does a different*
20 *dance move, backbend, handstand, or yoga pose while singing*
21 *something such as the* Star Spangled Banner.*)* **You see, man,**
22 **I'm for real, I'm not afraid of anything now! I am not afraid**
23 **of ... huh? What was that sound? Shhhh. Did you hear that?**
24 *(Suddenly points to the ground about five feet away. Speechless*
25 *for a moment then screams like a girl.)* **Agh, rattlesnake! Let's**
26 **get out of here.** *(Runs Off-stage down the mountain.)*

11. What's Wrong with Me?

1   What's wrong with me? I don't know. This is supposed
2   to be the greatest opportunity of my life. Everybody tells me
3   that. Why don't I feel anything except this heavy weight on
4   my shoulders? It's like here I am faced with this challenge
5   and all of a sudden all I want to do is ... just have fun. I'd
6   just like to do something fun and not have all this
7   responsibility. I know this is a great opportunity to succeed,
8   but at the same time it's an opportunity to fail, right? The
9   two go hand in hand. Failure and success. One can't exist
10 without the other. I mean, if there were no possibility of
11 failure, then why even try? And it's just that kind of
12 pressure that I'm tired of. Challenges. Hmph! That's been
13 my life for the last, I don't know, five, six years. A lot of
14 challenges. Nothing but challenges. I think maybe I'm just
15 burnt out. I know this whole thing is exciting for my family.
16 I can see that. Look at them. They love the idea that great
17 things can happen for me. That I can go far in life. But it's
18 hard to explain to them that I don't feel as excited as they
19 do anymore. I did. I really did in the beginning. But now? I
20 just feel empty inside. It's like my batteries need to be
21 charged. Like I'm running on reserve battery. I need a break.
22 But, I don't get one. Maybe I don't know what's best for me.
23 That's possible. What do you think? What's wrong with me?

12. Picture Perfect

1   I have a photographic memory. It's pretty cool. I can go
2 to an art museum, like this, and just pick out a couple of
3 paintings that I like and, *Bam!* I store them right up here.
4 *(Points to his head.)* Then, later when I go home, I put them
5 on my wall. In my imagination, of course. Like, say this is
6 my bedroom, right? My bed is right there and there's this
7 big space on the wall over here which is just right for this
8 painting by Van Gogh. I love this painting, don't you? I'm
9 between this one and *Cannon Rock* by Winslow Homer. You
10 don't know that one? Oh, it's one of my favorites. You have
11 to see it. It's in the American collection, well, obviously,
12 since Homer was an American. Did you know that a lot of
13 people consider him the greatest American painter of the
14 nineteenth century? Yeah, some people call him "The
15 American Monet." All of that doesn't matter to me though.
16 I just love *Cannon Rock* so much because I love the ocean
17 and I love the coast of Maine. That's where I'm from
18 originally. Maine. Yeah, *Cannon Rock* really captures the
19 coast for me. So I might hang this Van Gogh or *Cannon*
20 *Rock* in my bedroom. I haven't decided yet. It's funny
21 because people walk in my bedroom and all they see are
22 empty walls, but I've always got something up there in my
23 head. And every time I go to the museum I bring home
24 something new. Right now? Oh, right now when I look at the
25 wall across from my bed I see Edward Munch's *The Scream.*
26 I chose to put that one up because we just had final exams
27 and it was just unbelievable stress for me. Of course my
28 photographic memory does help me when I study. Yeah, it

1   comes in very handy, so I can't complain. However, if I don't
2   take the time to read, to go through the material, the
3   information won't magically make it into my brain. And
4   sometimes I rely on my ability to memorize too much and
5   wind up with a lot of information to cover in a very short
6   amount of time. So, yeah, I was pretty stressed out because
7   this term I definitely had a lot of information to cover and a
8   short amount of time to do it in. But it's over now and I did
9   really well, so I can relax. Yeah, I'm just spending the
10 summer in New York with my cousins. It's great. All of the
11 culture, the people. Very cool. Yeah, I love this museum. And
12 just walking around the city and the park. New York, for me,
13 I'd say it's picture perfect.

13. Road Runner

1   I'm in love with Road Runner. No, not the cartoon. Road
2 Runner is the number one runner on our girl's track team.
3 Abigail Saunders, a.k.a. "Road Runner." Abigail is amazing.
4 First of all ... can that girl run! Well, you probably already
5 figured that out I guess. But, wow, she is not just an
6 amazing runner. She is ... how can I say it? Amazing. Well,
7 for one thing I love her green hair. It's super long and silky.
8 And when she runs it just kind of swishes back and forth.
9 Like this. *(Shakes head.)* And she probably has the longest
10 legs of any girl I know. Long and tan. From all that running
11 in the sun. Abigail competes in triathlons, too. So she
12 swims and bikes and I hear that she's extremely fast.
13 Anyway, that's what they said in a feature article on her in
14 the school paper. I guess you could say that Abigail
15 Saunders is perfect. Or practically perfect, I guess, in every
16 way. It's like I said; I'm in love. *(Sighs.)* I haven't asked her
17 out yet, but I will. I will. I have a plan. Well, I have several
18 plans actually. I think about Abigail all the time and how we
19 are going to spend the rest of our lives together. So
20 naturally, I have to have a plan for asking her out. I know
21 it's just not going to happen. I have to make it happen.
22 Although, I do think sometimes something is just your
23 destiny and even my mother says, "If you don't have a plan,
24 your destiny has a plan for you." But I don't really get the
25 feeling in this case that destiny is planning to thrust me and
26 Abigail together into everlasting love. If it's going to happen,
27 there needs to be some work done on my part. See,
28 Abigail's pretty popular and, well, we sort of move in

1 different circles, if you know what I mean. We do have one
2 thing in common. I ride a bike, but I ride it to get to school.
3 Abigail rides hers in competitions. I just don't like
4 competition that much. I mean, not athletically anyway. I'm
5 more of a cerebral type. I think I'm drawn to Abigail because
6 she is my opposite. Obviously it's true that opposites
7 attract. So I'm hoping that in this case it will work both
8 ways. That is, as soon as Abigail gets to know me she'll be
9 attracted to me as much as I'm attracted to her. I almost
10 spoke to her once. Yes, I did. It was in the hall in front of Mr.
11 Aranson's Biology class on September fourteenth at two-
12 thirty-one pm. She dropped her books and I picked up one
13 of them for her. She said, "Thanks," and I was just about
14 to say something back, but by the time I looked up she was
15 gone already. I tell you she moves quick, that girl. But we
16 will meet one day. One day soon. And I'll probably say
17 something brilliant like, "Road Runner, I love you." Or,
18 "Marry me, Abigail Saunders." You know, something simple
19 like that.

14. Roller Coaster Rivalry

1   I spent the summer at the coaster park with my
2 brothers. We had a season pass and of course, they wanted
3 to go every day. They're twins. Thirteen years old and they
4 have to compete in everything. It's always, "Who runs the
5 fastest? Who gets the best grades? Who has the most
6 friends online?" And of course, "Who can ride the most
7 roller coasters in one day without getting sick?" It's all stuff
8 that won't get them in the Olympics of course, but it's like
9 my mother says, "As long as it keeps them off the streets."
10 So yeah, this summer we went to the coaster park just
11 about every day. I took them 'cause I can drive now and to
12 be honest, I didn't have anything better to do. I don't really
13 like roller coasters though, so I spent my time mostly just
14 kind of hanging out and people watching. Probably doesn't
15 sound too exciting to you, but I want to be a writer, so I like
16 watching people and listening to what they say. Not exactly
17 eavesdropping but, well, yeah, sort of eavesdropping, I
18 guess. I look at it sort of like recon though. Makes it seem
19 more exciting. So one day towards the end of summer, I was
20 walking through the section of the park with the carnival-
21 style games. You know, the part where they charge you an
22 arm and a leg to play some game where you might win a
23 stuffed animal or some superhero cape. I never in a million
24 years thought I would play one of those games because I
25 wouldn't have anything to do with either a stuffed animal or
26 a superhero cape, but one day ... one day last summer
27 everything changed. I was walking with the coin toss on the
28 left and the balloon darts on the right when I heard this

1   voice coming over the loud speaker from behind me. It was
2   a girl carnival barker with a voice like, well, it was like her
3   voice just floated to me like on an electric wave and woke
4   me up from a million years of slumber. She was saying,
5   "Step right up folks and I'll tell you a story of a little girl who
6   played this game and won a superhero cape. Now she's a
7   super girl and the same thing can happen to you. Then I'll
8   tell your story. Wouldn't you like that? Come on, folks. It only
9   takes two players to play this game. That's the square root
10 of four. That's five minus three," and so on and so on and
11 so on. I stopped dead in my tracks listening and then I did
12 a one-eighty. I had to know. Who was this funny, clever,
13 crazy girl who had such a way with words? So about an hour
14 later I met my brothers by the water coaster ride and they
15 almost didn't recognize me. I was wearing two superhero
16 capes and carrying a great, big, blue gorilla. And I was in
17 love. In love. And I never loved my little brothers more. How
18 could I know that their roller coaster rivalry could bring me
19 the woman of my dreams? And a big, blue gorilla, too.

15. Somethin' About Space

1   The topic of my oral report today is "Somethin' About
2 Space." You may have noticed that I'm not in school a lot
3 these days. I always tell everyone that's because I'm
4 working on my acting career. You know, getting parts in
5 student films, going on auditions. Out here in LA people
6 totally believe that, so that's just somethin' I say 'cause if
7 I tried to tell them the truth, they'd never buy it. You see,
8 I'm actually a teenage astronaut. Yep, I said astronaut. Go
9 ahead and laugh, but it's true. I'm working with the space
10 program on a top secret mission. I do realize that it sounds
11 unbelievable. Hey, I was just as skeptical as you the day the
12 space program approached me to offer me this exciting
13 opportunity for the first time. I was in the grocery store and
14 I couldn't figure out which chips to buy. There are so many
15 different kinds! That's when this lady from the space
16 program came up to me. She looked sort of like a sexy
17 librarian, you know. All decked out in horned rimmed
18 glasses and high heels. She says, "Young man, you look like
19 a real space cadet." I was like, "Excuse me, you talking to
20 me?" She says, "I certainly am. If you're willing to leave
21 everything behind that you ever thought to be true about
22 yourself and go where no man has ever gone before, I believe
23 you might have a lucrative career ahead of you." I didn't
24 know what the heck she was talking about, but I heard the
25 word "lucrative" and I knew what that meant — *(Looks over*
26 *at the teacher gratefully.)* thanks to Mrs. Roberts. So I was
27 like, "Dudette, I'm in!" Ever since then I've been in training.
28 And we'll embark on our first mission very soon. I'm not

1   sure exactly when because it's top secret stuff, man. If they
2   told me when it was going to take place, they might have to
3   kill me. So I'm like totally stoked. There's just somethin'
4   about space that is so ... intriguing. *(Proud of himself for*
5   *having thought of the word)* **Yeah, intriguing. I've been reading**
6   a lot about it lately and there's a lot of stuff I didn't even
7   realize. I'll bet I could teach you a few things that you didn't
8   know. Like ... well, like did you know Uranus was originally
9   called George's Star after King George III? I'd say that was
10   quite a compliment, wouldn't you? Oh, and here's another
11   cool thing. *(Walks to the window and points outside.)* **See that**
12   sunlight out there? Well, kids, that's some old light you're
13   lookin' at. The light hitting the earth right this second is
14   thirty thousand years old. Whoa, right? That one just totally
15   blows my mind. Also, did you know that our galaxy, the
16   Milky Way, is constantly moving super fast? So like in one
17   minute everybody in this room will be about 19 thousand
18   kilometers from where we were before. *(Looks over to Mrs.*
19   *Roberts.)* **Pretty awesome stuff, right? I thought so. This stuff**
20   is so awesome that I think there's a danger of overloading
21   some of our teenage minds with too much awesomeness at
22   once, so I'll keep my report short and to the point. I'm glad
23   I was able to step away from astronaut training to join you
24   today. Remember, not everyone can be a teenage astronaut,
25   but even the average Joe, or Josephine, can learn somethin'
26   about space.

16. Be Careful What You Wish For

1   Last year on Christmas day I was so happy. Mom and
2 Dad bought me everything I wanted. I got a bike, a new
3 basketball, and tons of cool clothes. It was great. I was so
4 happy that I stood in front of our giant Christmas tree,
5 squeezed my mom and dad super tight, and said, "I wish
6 every day were Christmas!" Boy, do I regret saying that!
7 How did I know that the wish fairy or whatever was ready to
8 grant my wish right at that very moment. Geez, Louise! Why
9 couldn't my wish fairy have come around some night when
10 I was wishing for a sports car or a date with Tiffany Potter,
11 or I don't know, just about anything. You're probably
12 wondering what I'm going on and on about. And actually,
13 it's a little hard to explain. But I'll try. You see about two
14 days after Christmas, two days after my wish, my mother
15 got a call. Her Great Aunt Tabitha was being kicked out of
16 her nursing home for unruly behavior and had to have a
17 place to go. Mom used to be real close to her Great Aunt
18 Tabitha, so of course there was only one place for her to go.
19 Our house. When I heard the news I felt a lot of things at
20 once. Mixed emotions as they say. I felt really, really sorry
21 for old Aunt Tabitha. I mean, what kind of jerks kick an old
22 lady out of an old folk's home, right? But then, just after I'd
23 think about that, I'd think, geez Louise, nothing's ever
24 gonna be the same around here. And boy, was that ever the
25 understatement of the year. Old Aunt Tabitha showed up
26 and our house got turned upside down. In more ways than
27 one. But we all love her, of course. She's sweet and she's
28 funny and she needs us. She really, really does. And it's nice

1   to be needed sometimes. But there's one thing about the
2   whole situation that's driving me mad. It's Christmas. See,
3   old Aunt Tabitha's pretty straight in her head except for one
4   department. And that one department is her daily calendar
5   is just a little bit off. Yep. Every day when she wakes up she
6   thinks it's Christmas and she will not listen to anybody who
7   tells her otherwise. So Aunt Tabitha's been with us since
8   December 28th and now we're going on Halloween. But do
9   we have a pumpkin in front of the house? Nope. We have
10 Christmas lights. They go with the Christmas tree that is
11 now a permanent fixture in the living room. And every night
12 after dinner we open presents, then wrap the same presents
13 before the next night. See, we found out that trying to tell
14 Aunt Tabitha it's not Christmas makes her very unhappy.
15 And when old Aunt Tabitha's unhappy, nobody's happy. So
16 Christmas it is. Ho, ho, ho.

17. I've Never Seen the Snow

1   I've never seen the snow. I grew up in Florida and my
2   mom always told me that we moved to Florida from
3   Colorado when I was a baby because I was allergic to the
4   snow. I know. Sounds weird, right? But hey, she's my mom
5   and I believed her. She also told me that my dad had died
6   before I was born and then she never ever talked about him
7   again. I'd ask questions, but she'd always avoid the subject.
8   But yesterday, we ran into this guy who knew my mom when
9   she was young and as it turns out he knew my dad, too.
10   Mom tried to act like she didn't remember him at first, but
11   it was obvious that she did. He asked my mom if she still
12   skied. I was like, "You ski?" She just looked the other way.
13   Then this guy says to me, "You must be so proud of your
14   dad and all the cool things he did." He's like, "Man, your
15   dad was a great guy." I said, "He was?" My mom says,
16   "You'll have to excuse us, but we're late and have to go."
17   She grabbed my arm and started to drag me away, but I
18   pulled back. I was like, "No, Mom. I want to know." She
19   looked like she was going to cry and she ran out of the
20   store. Part of me wanted to follow her, but the biggest part
21   of me wanted to stay. And I did. Pete, that was the guy's
22   name, seemed to feel really bad that he'd made my mom so
23   upset, but when he found out that I knew nothing about my
24   dad, I could tell he was glad he could share his story. See,
25   Pete and my dad were good friends, ski buddies. My dad as
26   it turns out was an extreme skier. I mean like a total, total
27   extreme skier. To tell you the truth I wasn't even sure what
28   that meant. Pete told me he'd come over to the house later

1   if my mom would let him and bring some pictures. He told
2   me he'd bought a summer house in Florida and had just
3   moved nearby. It took a lot of yelling, screaming, and crying,
4   but a few hours later Mom agreed to let Pete come. I felt so
5   excited but so confused. How could Mom let me go through
6   life not knowing who my dad was? How? She tried to explain
7   that she was afraid. Afraid that I'd follow in the footsteps of
8   my dad and that the same thing that happened to him would
9   happen to me. See, she loved my dad a lot I guess. And
10 after his accident in the Alps, she just couldn't get over it.
11 You know? It just changed her. And changed both of our
12 lives forever. Well, at least 'til now. See, I'm packing my stuff
13 and going to stay with Pete for a while in Colorado. It's a
14 decision that was hard to make, but it's something I have to
15 do. I have to get to know my dad in the only way I know. I
16 have to see the snow.

18. The Witness

1   What would you do if you knew that somebody at school
2   was getting bullied? By some really rotten people? People
3   you should probably be afraid of? Nothing? What can you
4   do? Maybe the guy who's getting bullied doesn't want you to
5   interfere. Maybe if you do interfere it will only make things
6   worse. What would you do? I'm asking because I've seen. I
7   know. I know someone who's getting bullied and it's making
8   me feel scared, guilty, and miserable all at once. I don't
9   really know this guy well enough to just go up and talk to
10 him, but I think that's what I'm going to have to do. Or tell
11 a guidance counselor or someone. The problem is I don't
12 really know the guidance counselors very well. And I'm kind
13 of afraid it will get out that I told. Then what will happen to
14 me? I just don't want to go on the internet and see our
15 school in the news 'cause something disastrous happened
16 with this kid. You know? You see that all the time, right? I
17 just don't think I could live with myself if something
18 happens to him and I could have done something about it.
19 In a way, I wish I just didn't know. You know that old saying,
20 "What you don't know, won't hurt you." Maybe it's true. I
21 wish I just didn't know. Then everything would be fine,
22 right? Yeah, right. Is it OK to know something like this and
23 not do anything about it? I mean, people do it all the time,
24 don't they? I mean, there are homeless people that we see
25 in the street and people getting treated unfairly in the
26 justice system, or facing illness and disease without health
27 care. We don't always do something about that, do we?
28 Sometimes we don't even want to know. It's like, you go

1   online and you could read about poverty in the Appalachians
2   or you can read about what some pop star wore on the red
3   carpet. What are you gonna read? Right? Well, sometimes
4   things are easy to avoid like that and then sometimes
5   whether you like it or not you're a witness. A witness to
6   some injustice. Like bullying. Then, what are you going to
7   do?

19. Spring Cleaning

1   I like holey underwear! Mom! Do not throw those out!

2   *(Exasperated)* How old will I have to be before you stop

3   breaking and entering into my room and worrying about

4   what's happening with my stuff? I happen to like having a

5   pile of dirty clothes! It's my choice. I have the right to a pile

6   of dirty laundry. Do I have to take you to court? Do I have

7   to become an emancipated minor? I'm warning you, put that

8   dirty pair of jeans down or I'll take steps. I will. Even if I

9   have to live in a cardboard box under the Fifth Street Bridge.

10 At least I'll be independent. Don't do it, Mom. Don't take my

11 dirty laundry. I'm serious. You're testing me. You really are.

12 OK, I'm warning you. I don't like it. I don't. *(Watches his mom*

13 *leave the room with the clothes in tow. Looks at the audience.)*

14 Reverse psychology. Works every time.

20. The Cure for Insomnia

1   My dad's a teen novelist wannabe. Well, I mean, he
2 actually has written several novels, so he really is a novelist,
3 but it's just that nothing's been published yet. But he just
4 keeps on trying. His latest novel is about a teen spy who
5 pretends to be some big shot's kid so he can find out
6 secrets about our alien enemies and save the world or
7 something like that. I really, really want to read his novel,
8 but every time I start to read it I get so sleepy. I just nod
9 off. It's a total cure for insomnia. It never fails. Dad asked
10 me the other day, "Do you think it's gonna make us a
11 million bucks?" I said, "Oh sure, Dad, it's great. I'm not
12 done with it yet, but loving every minute of it." What I really
13 wanted to say is, "If you could bottle it, it would."

21. I'm Just Sayin'

1   You're obsessed with him. You are, too. You are not just
2   a normal fan. OK, listen, what do you think? You've seen all
3   of his movies at least twenty-five times each. At least fifty?
4   OK, then how can you argue with me? I'm just sayin' it's
5   not healthy. You need a life. You do not have a life. You fill
6   every moment just thinking about some guy you'll never
7   have. Oh, really? Like what? What else do you do? OK, sure
8   you go to gymnastics once a week. I hate to tell you this,
9   but you suck at gymnastics. You need to get another sport.
10 I'm just sayin' you're wasting your time. Yeah, I've seen you.
11 We've all seen you and if you ask anybody they'll tell you the
12 same thing. Well, that is if they're honest. Not everybody
13 tells it like it is. That's one thing you have to watch out for.
14 Like your parents. They're never gonna tell you you're not
15 good enough. Your parents? They're too nice. No, no, they're
16 not liars. Not in the usual sense of the word. I'm just sayin'
17 that they'd go to the ends of the earth not to hurt you.
18 That's all. So you can't take them seriously when they tell
19 you stuff like that. Deb, you are not going to make it to the
20 Olympics. I'm just sayin' they're just setting you up for
21 failure, that's all. Yeah, you're lucky that you have a friend
22 like me to help you see things the way they are. I'm just
23 sayin', well, you know. It would be a better world if everyone
24 could have a friend like me.

22. Leaf It to Me

1   Our assignment in business class was to come up with
2 a business that had a niche market, could be a source of
3 revenue for a high school student, and would have a positive
4 impact on the environment. The business I created is called
5 "Leaf It to Me." It's a service I offer to people with yards
6 where I bring my rake and a wheelbarrow and I clean up the
7 leaves in their yards. It's a cool business model because I
8 don't need anything but my wheelbarrow and rake. See, the
9 deal is that I will either pile their leaves up in a convenient
10 place for them to turn into compost which is basically
11 fertilizer. Then I'll come back on a follow-up visit and spread
12 the compost around. It adds nutrients to the soil, improving
13 its composition and improving drainage as well. If the
14 customer doesn't want to keep a pile of leaves in the yard
15 for compost, I haul the leaves away to my house, where my
16 dad lets me make compost piles in the backyard. The
17 overhead for my business is very low. The cost of the rake
18 and the wheelbarrow. Not only is the compost good for the
19 environment but using a rake instead of a leaf blower is too.
20 You may not have been aware of this, but gas-powered leaf
21 blowers are a source of air and noise pollution. So if I can
22 convince everyone on my street to cross over to raking, I'll
23 be helping us all to breathe cleaner air. Of course, a lot of
24 my customers would already have lawn service, but I'm a
25 specialty service, which is kind of nice, too. See, if their
26 lawn guy isn't due to come for another day or two but the
27 leaves are out of hand, I can just take care of that one thing
28 for them, without causing a lot of ruckus in their yard. So

1 anyway, I got an A+ from Mr. Farley, my business teacher.
2 And I think I'm actually going to give the business a try.
3 See, I even had this T-shirt made up with "Leaf It to Me" on
4 the back. Didn't cost too much, but it did increase my
5 overhead slightly. Looks cool, though, doesn't it?

23. Why Now?

1   My parents just told me last night that they're getting a
2 divorce. All I could think of was, "Why now?" This is my
3 senior year of high school. Isn't this supposed to be one of
4 the best years of my life? Don't they care about me at all? I
5 don't know where all this came from anyway. It seems to me
6 like we were all getting along just fine. Great actually. Sure,
7 they fight off and on, but it always blows over. Why the
8 sudden urge to go their separate ways, split up our family,
9 and destroy my life? When I told Terry he said, "I bet you a
10 million dollars that one of your parents is seeing someone
11 else." I was like, my parents? No way. Not "My mom and
12 dad. They wouldn't do that." I couldn't imagine that with
13 either one of them. Terry thinks that because that's what his
14 father did. He met some lady at work and, *Bam!* One day he
15 just dropped the bomb on them all and split. *(Sighs.)* I don't
16 know, maybe that's it. My parents wouldn't give me any
17 details. They just said they both loved me and wanted to be
18 good parents, but they had grown apart and couldn't stay
19 together anymore. Maybe Terry's right. Maybe that's what
20 they meant when they said they'd "grown apart". Well, that
21 would be just perfect. Here it is my senior year when I'm
22 supposed to be dating and stuff and one of my parents has
23 been out trying to one up me behind my back. Why should
24 I have all the fun, right? Geez, why can't they just let me
25 have my turn. If they wanted to act like teenagers, they
26 could have waited until I went away to college next year.
27 Why now?

24. What Are You Going to Be When You Grow Up?

1   I wish my parents would decide on what they want to be
2 when they grow up! I'm serious. It's always changing with
3 them and it always seems to impact me. How? Like one day
4 I'm sitting there eating a cheese pizza with Tony when my
5 dad walks in and announces he's going to school in the
6 evenings to become a raw food chef. I was like, "Cool, Dad!"
7 Little did I know that I would start coming home to raw
8 meals every night of my life. I mean, they're not that bad,
9 but I'm like "Hey, this was Dad's decision, not mine! How
10 come I can't just put a frozen dinner in the microwave?" But
11 Mom says we need to support each other, so we do. We sit
12 and eat zucchini pasta and pretend it's spaghetti with
13 meatballs or something. Oh, yeah, and that's not all. Last
14 year my mom decided she wanted to go to beauty school
15 and learn how to cut hair and all that. My sister Angela had
16 really short hair, so she was no fun. But me? I had hair down
17 to my butt in those days. Yeah, it was awesome. So,
18 anyway, Mom tried every style in the book on me before the
19 year was out 'til I ended up with this. Hey, dude! I'm not
20 bald! This is called a close shave. So, yeah, it's not so bad.
21 Yeah, I like it. It just ticked me off, man, 'cause after all that
22 sacrifice on my part, my hair and all, my mom dropped out
23 of school. Yeah, just like that. She decided the whole hair
24 thing was just a superficial art and she joined some group
25 of yogis or something. Yeah, it's whacked. Oh, well. It's like
26 I'm telling you. I wish my parents would make up their
27 minds. And I wish they'd grow up.

25. Foreclosure

1   I'm sitting there in English today and Mr. Gobel is
2   talking about all these vocabulary words. You know, words
3   we should know before we leave the ninth grade. And I'm
4   sitting there the whole time thinking of only one word.
5   Foreclosure. Yep. Foreclosure. I hate that word, 'cause
6   that's what's happening to me. To my family. We have five
7   days to get out of our house. We're being evicted by the
8   sheriff. What happened? Life is what happened. At least
9   that's what my dad says. My mom was sick for a while and
10   lost her job. My dad didn't have health insurance and had
11   to have an operation. It was just like one disaster after
12   another for a while. And now this. At least we have my
13   mom's Aunt Reba to go to. She's letting us live with her for
14   a while 'til we get back on our feet again. So I'll be leaving
15   in five days. Yeah, I'll be going to Alabama. Never been there
16   before. Don't know what it will be like, actually. I just know
17   we're selling or giving away our stuff and taking only what
18   we can pack in our car. We can't afford to move our stuff.
19   My mom's just terrified our car will break down before we
20   get there. I'm sure it will. The way things are going and all.
21   Oh, well. What can you do? I tried to get a job and help out,
22   but Mom and Dad wanted me to concentrate on school. I
23   don't think my "salary" as a fast food fryer would have
24   saved the day, anyway. I'll miss our house. I'll miss this
25   neighborhood and ... I hate to say it, but I'll even miss this
26   school. Yeah, as much as it sucks I'll still be sorry to have
27   to go. Yeah, and I'll miss you, too. I shouldn't even have to
28   say that, dummy. Of course I'll miss you most of all.

26. Timing Is Everything

1   Timing is everything, man. For instance, I was planning
2 to go to a concert tonight with some friends. Then I walked
3 in the door after school and saw my dad reading the mail. I
4 said, "Hey, Dad" and started upstairs. But Dad said, "Just
5 a minute, Eric." I stopped dead in my tracks when I heard
6 his tone of voice. I've heard it before and it's usually not
7 good. So I turned around and said, "Yes, sir" in my most
8 obedient voice. And Dad said, "Mail, just came. This one's
9 for you. Hope you don't mind that I opened it." I walked over
10 to look at it and almost died. It was a letter from the
11 Clarence County Sheriff's Traffic Enforcement Department.
12 It consisted of a series of photographs of me, driving my
13 dad's car and running a red light at Forty-First and Vine.
14 Yeah, it was really crappy timing. Dad says, "Son, I think
15 you'd better call your friends and let them know the
16 concert's been cancelled. For you, that is." I started to say
17 "Aw, Dad!" but I thought better of it. I was so disappointed
18 I felt like I couldn't breathe. Then to add insult to injury, my
19 dad says, "Maybe Scotty next door will buy your concert
20 ticket. I know his mother said he wanted to go." Scotty!
21 He's practically my archenemy which is why I didn't invite
22 him to go in the first place. But Dad was probably just
23 trying to help, in his weird, mean way. Help me put together
24 the fine to pay for my traffic violation that is. Running a red
25 light can cost an arm and a leg.

27. Grounded ... Again

1   I haven't been smoking! I told you, Mom. I stopped doing
2   that the minute you caught me and grounded me and all
3   that. I did! I swear. Cross my heart and hope to die. Yes. Of
4   course. Do you think that after that terrific lecture you gave
5   me about the many, many serious reasons I should not
6   smoke, that I would be stupid enough to take even one puff?
7   You what? You have evidence? What is this? A court of law?
8   What friend of mine sent you a video from the party last
9   Friday night? Who? Tell me. Who? Whoever it was, they're
10   not a "friend" of mine. Don't even use that word. No, I don't
11   want to see it. Why don't you just post it online? Then
12   everyone in the neighborhood can watch it and just tell me
13   about it later. Yeah, yeah, the point is I was smoking. Only
14   a few puffs. No, I do not want to see the video. What did they
15   do, follow me around the whole night? Never mind. So,
16   what? Am I grounded? Again? Two weeks? Two weeks? Does
17   that mean I can't go to Karen's birthday party at the beach?
18   Mom! Please! I have to go to Karen's party. I love her! I do.
19   No, I know that I shouldn't have been smoking. I know that
20   I shouldn't have lied to you about it. I'm sorry! I'm really,
21   really sorry. Mom, please! Please let me go to Karen's party.
22   You can ground me for a month if you just let me go. No,
23   I'm not trying to tell you what to do. I know, I know, you
24   make the rules. I know I live in your house. Mom! Can't we
25   work something out? What if I promise never, ever to smoke
26   again for the rest of my life? Why won't you believe me? I
27   mean it. Can't you see, I've changed. What changed me?
28   This changed me? I want to go to Karen's party! I mean, I

1   don't want to keep getting in trouble. It's just ... not right.
2   If I keep getting grounded I'll lose my friends. I'll lose Karen.
3   She could go out with any guy in the school, but she picked
4   me. If I don't go to her party I'll be letting her down. She'll
5   ... she'll never speak to me again. *(Starts to cry.)* **Why don't**
6   **you ... why? Why do you hate me so much? You're about to**
7   **ruin my life and you don't even care. My whole life, at every**
8   **school, I've had no friends at all. You know that's true. Now**
9   **finally, at this school, people like me. I fit in. No, they're not**
10 **bad kids. They're not. They're my friends. If you gave them**
11 **a chance, Mom, maybe you'd like them. If you got to know**
12 **them, I mean. You won't even let me bring anyone over to**
13 **the house. And now I can't go out. Mom! Please, please.**
14 **Why are you doing this to me?**

28. The Breakup — Alonzo's Story

1   I finally did it. I broke up with Tara. Yup. I've been
2 wanting to for a long time now, but today I finally got up the
3 nerve. This morning before first period. How did she take it?
4 How do think she took it? She was devastated. I was her
5 first boyfriend, dude! She was totally, madly in love with me.
6 She was always saying it all the time. "I love you, Alonzo. I
7 love you so much." It was starting to make me nervous. No,
8 I mean, Tara is hot and sweet and all that, but I'm not ready
9 for love. I don't even want to think about love. I just want
10 to think about what I'm doing on Saturday night. Anyway, it
11 was getting kind of embarrassing. The way she just
12 worshipped the ground that I walked on. And that love stuff,
13 too. We'd be walking in the hall at school and I'd drop her
14 off at her class and she would be like, "Love you, bye." It
15 was like she wanted every other girl in school to know that
16 I was hers and hers alone. It felt like I was in prison or
17 something. I just want to have fun. But yeah, I do feel bad
18 for Tara. Like I said, she's devastated. I never saw anybody
19 cry so hard in my life. It kind of made me sorry we ever went
20 out in the first place. I mean, I don't want to ruin anybody's
21 life. I'm too young to feel this guilty. Women! It's like my dad
22 says, "You can't live with 'em, and you can't live without
23 'em." Oh well, I'm just glad it's over. Time to move on,
24 man. Right?

29. The Many Lives of Stephanie Steuben Skylake

1   I'd like to tell you the story of the many lives of
2   Stephanie Steuben Skylake. My sister's story, that is. You
3   see, my sister's name is Stephanie Steuben Skylake and
4   well, she actually has only one life. In reality. However, in her
5   mind, in her fantasies, she has, let's say, several. You see,
6   a few years ago, apparently Stephanie started thinking
7   about how different her life might be if she'd taken a
8   different path or made a different decision. You know, when
9   facing some fork in the road, so to speak. Like if she'd made
10   a different choice in some life-defining moment. Or like,
11   even if my parents or I had made a different choice. Or my
12   other brothers and sisters, you know. It's like she started to
13   see life as this total experience of cause and effect. And
14   then it was as if she just became obsessed with it, you
15   know. The great "what if." It was just so compelling for her
16   to imagine what might have been or what might be. So like
17   I said, a few years ago she started thinking about all of this
18   and couldn't stop. I think she was actually kind of miserable
19   at that time because we had just moved to Valencia and
20   Stephanie was just bored out of her mind. No, not Valencia,
21   Spain. Valencia, California. She didn't know anybody and my
22   parents were broke from having just moved our whole troop
23   across the country from Miami. So Stephanie started
24   thinking, "What would I be doing today if we hadn't moved?"
25   Apparently that's when she took out her journal and started
26   writing. Her first journal entry starts, "Today I'm going to
27   start writing about the many lives of Stephanie Steuben
28   Skylake." And then she went on from there and filled about

1 fifteen journals. Yeah, fifteen! Like I said, it became an
2 obsession. She'd come home from school every day and
3 write about her "real" day and then about the other days she
4 might be having or could be having, if ... you know. If Mom
5 and Dad had won the lottery. If she'd gone away to boarding
6 school. The variations on Stephanie's life were endless. And
7 it became a big job keeping up with it all. After dinner she'd
8 go straight to her room and we wouldn't see her again all
9 night. We all thought she was doing her homework until she
10 brought her report card home. It was the first time she had
11 ever gotten a D. Mom and Dad got concerned. And that's
12 when they did a little snooping in her room. I don't say it was
13 right, but I'm glad they did. I care about my little sister and
14 I think she needed help. Sometimes parents just have to
15 interfere. So now Stephanie is seeing a counselor and she's
16 doing better, I think. My parents have enrolled her in classes
17 and stuff, so that she'll make some friends and be busy and
18 all that. She's like, taking gymnastics and art classes, too.
19 And it seems to be helping a lot. She still keeps a journal,
20 but she locks it in her desk drawer at night. She's still a
21 little bit hurt that her privacy was invaded, you know. But
22 still, I think she knows it was for the best. She knows my
23 parents love her and want her to have a good life. One, real,
24 true life, not thirty-five imaginary ones. So, it's all good. But
25 sometimes I worry. I'll be talking to Stephanie and I see this
26 far away look in her eyes. I'll say, "Steph, are you listening?"
27 She always says she is, but I don't think so. I think she's
28 somewhere far away, living one of the many lives of
29 Stephanie Steuben Skylake.

30. Taking Turns, Melting Down

1   My Auntie Frieda is so rude. She hardly ever calls our
2 house, but when she does she usually says somethin' nasty.
3 Like, "Who's in rehab this week?" Well, I know somebody
4 usually is, but she doesn't have to come out and say it that
5 way. She could be nice. My momma says it's just not in her
6 nature to be nice. Oh, well, it's true you know, in my family
7 we have a lot of issues. Sometimes it seems like we have
8 more than most folks, but my counselor says that's not the
9 case. My counselor says that a lot of families have a lot of
10 issues. Only difference is, they don't always do something
11 about them, whereas in my family, we do. I remember the
12 first time I went to rehab. I was so scared. I thought I was
13 never gonna come out. But it was good, you know. It was all
14 good. I mean, sure it was tough. I missed my momma so
15 bad. She came to visit me every night, but I missed her all
16 day long. And I missed my friends. But I don't suppose they
17 were real friends anyway, since it was kind of their fault that
18 I ended up in rehab in the first place. Well, it wasn't exactly
19 their fault. I do take responsibility. That's important, you
20 know. But my "friends", or the kids I thought were my
21 friends, they introduced me to stuff. They encouraged me.
22 And I just wasn't strong enough to say no. It was that whole
23 thing of wanting to fit in, I guess. Rehab really helped me to
24 see that. How I had issues and I needed to work on myself.
25 It was real good, but I sure don't want to go back. I've been
26 there two times since that first time, and believe me, that is
27 enough. It was kind of weird though, 'cause one time I
28 wasn't out of there more than a week when my brother Jerry

1   went in. So I went with Momma on visiting hour once, but I
2   couldn't handle it. Man, was I paranoid. I was terrified that
3   the techs might get confused and not let me out. I could
4   hardly breathe, until I left that night. Poor Jerry. He took it
5   a lot harder than me, though. He just wouldn't face the fact
6   that he had to work the program, you know. And that he
7   couldn't come home until he did. That's why he didn't get to
8   come home for a long time. When I saw him again, I
9   practically didn't recognize him. The whole experience was
10 really, really hard on my poor momma. It just about tore my
11 momma up. Matter of fact, she had to go to rehab as soon
12 as Jerry came out. Just so she could recuperate, you know?
13 Plus, Jerry's counselors told her that she had some sort of
14 enabling issues or something like that she had to work out.
15 I think it was a lot of garbage, but they said some sort of co-
16 dependency stuff was going on. I didn't pay much attention
17 to it. But I did go visit Momma every single day. I hated her
18 not being at home. It made me so sad. It hurt so much. I
19 just couldn't go a day without seeing momma, so I got there
20 no matter what. One time I missed the bus and had to walk
21 five miles in the rain. But it felt good. Yeah, it felt good to do
22 something for Momma for a change. *(Gets quiet thinking about*
23 *it.)* Yeah, in my family, it's like we've just been taking turns
24 melting down, I guess. But at least we do something about
25 it and I know we'll be OK in the end. Yeah, bro. It's tough.
26 It is. But in the end, we're there for each other and ... it's all
27 good.

31. The Babysitter

1   *(Sitting on the couch watching TV)* **Just where do you think**
2   **you're going missy? Sweetie, I've got eyes in the back of my**
3   **head, so don't try to tiptoe away and not answer me.** *(The*
4   *child appears at his side.)* **So, are you going to tell me where**
5   **you were going at** *(Looks at watch.)* **half an hour past your**
6   **bedtime? Hmmmm, little Miss Muffet? I see. You were going**
7   **for a drink of water. OK. Go ahead, but don't dilly-dally, you**
8   **hear? One quick drink and it's back under the sheets. No ifs**
9   **ands or buts.** *(Phone rings.)* **Yallo. Hey Walter, wuz up? Naw**
10   **man, I can't. I'm stuck babysitting the brats. Yeah, my**
11   **parents went to the movies. They figure somebody's got to**
12   **have a life, so it might as well be them, right? Yeah, that's**
13   **parental logic alright. So are you guys going out again**
14   **tomorrow night? Well, if you do, don't forget to call me. I'm**
15   **not booked at the kiddy ranch tomorrow night. Yeah, I'm a**
16   **free man. Yeah. Later.** *(Looks over to the left and the child is*
17   *standing there in tears.)* **Hey, Miss Muffet what happened to**
18   **you? What? What are you saying? Honey, I can't understand**
19   **you. Stop crying, sweetie, and tell your big brother what's**
20   **wrong. What? You're not a brat? Well, of course you're not.**
21   **Who said you were? I did?** *(Thinks about it for a minute.)* **Oh.**
22   **I did.** *(Feeling bad)* **I'm sorry, sweetie. I shouldn't have said**
23   **that. But you shouldn't have been listening to my phone call**
24   **either. If you had gone back to bed like I told you, you**
25   **wouldn't have heard that, now would you? No, you would not**
26   **have. That's why you need to do what you're told. But I was**
27   **wrong too, sweetie. I should never have said what I said.**
28   **You, little cupcake, are definitely not a brat. I didn't really**

1   mean that you were, but I'm sorry. Can you forgive me?
2   *(Kisses her on the head.)* **Now get back in bed.** *(Gives her a*
3   *stern look. Then softly)* **Sweet dreams, cupcake. Good night.**

32. Opposing Goals

1   I'm so nervous. My dad and I have a one-on-one tonight
2 at eight thirty. A one-on-one. You know, an appointment to
3 talk. Well, when your dad is the head coach of the number
4 one hockey team in the state, yeah, you do need an
5 appointment to talk to him. Unfortunately. *(Sighs.)* I am just
6 totally dreading it, 'cause what I have to say is not going to
7 be easy. Well, my dad, like I said, he coaches hockey. But
8 like my mother says, "He doesn't just coach hockey; he
9 lives, breathes, eats, and sleeps hockey." Hockey is my
10 dad's life. And, I know that's what he wants for my life. For
11 me to be a great hockey player. And I am pretty good, but
12 ... it's not what I want to do. It's not my dream. My dream?
13 Well, you'll probably laugh. Promise? OK. My dream is to be
14 an Olympic figure skater. Yes, I said figure skater. See, I
15 told you you'd laugh. No, no, it's OK. Go ahead. Believe me
16 it's nothing to be laughed at by you when I'll probably get
17 killed by my dad later tonight. Yes, that's what I'm planning
18 to tell him. I'm going to tell him what I've been wanting to
19 tell him since I was about *(Holds his hand to his knee.)* this
20 high. But, I know he'll be ... well, super mad. He ... just
21 won't understand. Believe me, I know my dad. Why do you
22 think I kept my love for skating a secret for so long? I know
23 my dad and I know my dad's temper. He'll be furious. He
24 just won't understand how I feel. Hmmmm? How I feel is
25 like if I can't figure skate, I'll die. Seriously. When I play
26 hockey I feel like a fish out of water. I can do it, but it
27 doesn't come naturally. I don't have the passion that I see
28 in the other guys. But when I'm skating I feel ... so free. So

1   one hundred percent me. And that's a Me that my dad has

2   never seen. It's almost like he doesn't really know me at all.

3   But *(Looks at his watch.)* in about one hour ... he will.

33. Stand-Up

1   "My mother is soooo overprotective. How overprotective
2   is she? When I went to go try out for football, she wrapped
3   me in bubble wrap." That was the line that brought down
4   the house. Seriously. They were rolling in the aisles. It was
5   the best night of stand-up I've ever done. Boy, I wish you'd
6   been there. I wish somebody I knew had been there, so they
7   could validate me, you know. 'Cause I know that it's hard to
8   believe, but I killed. I really, truly killed. When am I doing it
9   again? Um. Monday night. They're having a contest and I
10 just made it under the wire to register. What? What do you
11 mean I can't do it Monday night? What? That's this Monday
12 night? I thought that was like in December or something.
13 Ah, geez. Toby's Bar Mitzvah is this Monday night. Well, I
14 just can't go. No, not to the comedy club. I just can't go to
15 Toby's Bar Mitzvah. So let Mom kill me. If I miss this
16 contest, life won't be worth living anyway. Melissa, I'm
17 serious. This contest is huge. And I can't get my money
18 back. My registration money. It was non-refundable. I don't
19 want to tell you how much. No, I'm not telling. OK, it was
20 one hundred bucks. OK, OK, two hundred bucks. Yes,
21 Melissa, it's expensive to have a dream. And, you know it's
22 like Dad always says, "Money makes money." See, now you
23 can't ever tell me I didn't learn anything from Dad. What do
24 you mean where did I get two hundred dollars from? From
25 my college fund, of course. Yes, I have access to it. I've
26 always only made deposits, but as it turns out I was
27 perfectly capable of making a withdrawal. So I did. Melissa,
28 I am never going to college. Melissa, you're not listening to

1 me. Stand-up is what I want to do. It is what I'm going to
2 do. Hey, you're my sister, you're supposed to be on my side,
3 right? So stop acting like Mom or Dad. *(Sighs.)* You know
4 what? I think it's good that this happened. I think there's no
5 time like the present to get the truth out in the open. You
6 know, lay it all on the line. Toby's Bar Mitzvah came along
7 to give me the push that I needed. I mean, obviously the fact
8 that it fell on the night of the contest is not a mistake. Like
9 Grandpa says, Melissa, *(Imitating an old man)* "In life, there
10 are no mistakes." This is a sign. This is it. The universe is
11 telling me, Sis. It's shouting it out loud. *(Imitating the*
12 *universe — however it may sound)* "Aaron Stein, the moment
13 has come, son, for you to stand up." *(Then in an imitation of*
14 *Groucho Marx)* In more ways than one, if you know what I
15 mean."

34. The Real Thing

1   What do you mean I'm too young to date? I'm thirteen.
2   That's way old enough. You're just jealous, Dad! Yeah,
3   jealous. Go ahead and laugh. You know it's true. I may be
4   "only thirteen", but I've found my soulmate and let's face it,
5   Dad, you haven't had a date in about a hundred years. Mom
6   divorced you how long ago? And you're still not remarried?
7   Yeah, I know you don't want to listen to this. You don't want
8   to face the truth. But you need to. Yeah, you do. You're a
9   miserable, unhappy guy and you can't stand me because I'm
10   everything you're not. What is that? Happy and in love. Yes,
11   I may be only thirteen, but I am also happy and I'm in love.
12   Yes, I do. I do know what love is. What makes you think I
13   don't? My age? Well that proves right there that you don't
14   know anything about love. Love is ... it's ... you know,
15   ageless. Love is ... timeless. Love is for an eternity. Didn't
16   you ever love someone when you were young? Before Mom?
17   Try to remember what it was like. Try to think about what it
18   would be like to be in my shoes. Dad, please. I'm sorry
19   about what I said about you being jealous. I know you're
20   not. I know you really do want the best for me. But Dad, I'm
21   telling you. I'm in love and this is ... totally ... the real thing.

35. It's the Little Things

1   What was it that drove Cindy and I apart? Well, it wasn't
2 one thing. It was a lot of little things. Like what? Well, she
3 had this way of ... well ... nose talking. *(Imitates her.)* Like
4 this. "Frank, what movie do you want to see?" or "Frank, do
5 you think I look fat in these pants?" Oh, yeah, that was
6 another "little" thing. She was always asking me if she
7 looked fat. That gets tiring after a while. Always having to
8 say, "No, Cindy, you look great." Or "Of course not, Cindy,
9 you're the thinnest girl in the room." You know, junk like
10 that.
11   Well, no, that wasn't all. Let's see there was the slurping
12 and burping when she ate. No, I'm not exaggerating. And
13 eating my food before she even started eating her own. I'd
14 be like, "Cindy, if you wanted lasagna why didn't you order
15 it?" She always thought I was joking. She always thought
16 that I thought everything she did was super cute. And I
17 guess I did at first. I mean, when we first started dating all
18 her little annoying habits were like, cute to me. I even called
19 her my "Cute Little Mosquito." But sadly, what was cute in
20 the beginning quickly grew very annoying. Yes, my Cute
21 Little Mosquito became "That Annoying Little Gnat." And I
22 guess that's when I knew it was over for me.

36. The Old Gang

1   *(Talking to someone sitting next to him at a party)* **Yeah,**
2 **Callie and I can't believe we'll be back in the old**
3 **neighborhood tomorrow. Yeah, we can't wait. Uh huh. It's**
4 **gonna be great to see the old gang. Well, I mean gang like**
5 **in bunch of kids, you know. Not like gang as in** *(Makes*
6 *gangster pose.)* **"gang." Yeah, it's gonna be great. I can't wait**
7 **to see Bucky Schriver.** *(Calls across the room to Callie.)* **Hey,**
8 **Callie, remember little Bucky Schriver?** *(To person sitting next*
9 *to him again)* **Bucky Schriver was this tiny little kid that**
10 **could con anybody about anything. One time I told him I**
11 **wanted to get rid of my freckles, so the next day he comes**
12 **over with a bottle of homemade "Freckle Removing**
13 **Solution" he offered to sell me for five bucks. I bought it and**
14 **did what he said. Waited for a full moon to slather it on and**
15 **turned around seven times before saying, "Freckles be**
16 **gone." Turns out it was just some olive oil he found in his**
17 **mom's cupboard. Poured it in a jar, found a sucker, and**
18 **made a quick five bucks. Of course I threatened to beat him**
19 **up when I found out. But I wasn't much of a fighter, so that**
20 **never happened. Naw, I was a passive type even then. Yeah,**
21 **it's gonna be a lot of fun going back in time. Sort of like a**
22 **time machine, except I expect that nobody will look the**
23 **same. That will be strange. Maybe I won't even recognize**
24 **little Bucky. By now he might be six feet tall. I think they'll**
25 **all recognize me, since I never could get rid of these**
26 **freckles. I wonder what Bucky will try to con me about this**
27 **time. Yeah, I'll bet he's just the same. You know what they**
28 **say, "You can't make a leopard change its spots."**

37. Never Go Bowling

1   Well, it's over. Daisy and I broke up. Yes, I am dead
2   serious. Nope, she broke up with me. Because I couldn't
3   bowl. Yup. Not making it up. We've been inseparable for two
4   years. We've gone everywhere together. And I mean
5   everywhere. Like? The Grand Canyon, Niagara Falls, Navy
6   Pier in Chicago, Ruby Falls in Tennessee. Mount Rushmore,
7   and Mount Everest. We've played tennis, played chess,
8   played cards, gone mountain climbing, snowboarding, ice
9   skating, skydiving, parasailing, and we've seen just about
10 every movie that's ever been made ... I think, but for some
11 strange reason, until last night, we never, ever made it into
12 a bowling alley. I wasn't intentionally avoiding the sport, it
13 just never came up. Then last night, Daisy's cousin BC was
14 in town and he invited us to go bowling. And BC is a bowler.
15 And when I say a bowler, I mean a champion, bring your
16 own ball kind of bowler. And well, Daisy, as we all know, is
17 very competitive. So I wasn't that surprised when she got
18 upset when my bowling score tanked, causing us to lose
19 every game we played against BC and BC's friend Ted. Who,
20 I might add, just for the record, is also a champion, bring
21 your own ball kind of guy. OK? OK. Well, anyway, like I said,
22 I wasn't surprised when Daisy got upset, but I was a little
23 surprised at how extremely upset she got. I mean she went
24 bowling ballistic. I thought she was going to go through the
25 roof. When I threw my last gutter ball it was like, the last
26 straw for her and she just lost it. I'm telling you, she ranted
27 and raved, she jumped up and down, and then ... she
28 dumped me. Right there. On the spot. In no uncertain

1   terms. With ... gusto and gall. I'm telling you Tommy, listen
2   to your older brother when I tell you there's a lesson to be
3   learned somewhere in all of this. I'm just not sure what it is
4   at the moment. But since last night I've walked the floors.
5   I've been walking and thinking and thinking and walking and
6   walking and thinking some more and I think I've narrowed it
7   down to two pieces of advice that I'd like to pass on. *(In his*
8   *most serious voice)* "Never go bowling unless you absolutely
9   have to," and if you do, "Never go up against a guy who
10 brings his own ball."

38. Muddy and Lee

1   My little brother Lee managed to convince my parents
2   that he was old enough to stay home alone last night. He
3   really, really didn't want to see me in the school play, I
4   guess. I was sort of disappointed, but nevertheless, I went
5   on with the show. So Lee stays home and as it turns out two
6   guys broke out of the penitentiary, which is only about ten
7   miles away from our house. So all night long they had these
8   helicopters out looking for these guys and going over and
9   over our neighborhood with their search lights. And then
10   they actually had dogs out running through our yard. You
11   know, police dogs. Turns out these guys were actually hiding
12   in our shed. Muddy, our dog, was barking her head off
13   'cause she could smell the dogs. But when the police fired
14   a shot, Muddy went running to her usual hiding place.
15   Straight under my bed. It's so funny, because the play was
16   a musical and the band was playing so loud we never even
17   heard the helicopters. And by the time we left, the whole
18   thing was over and we didn't have a clue. But when we came
19   in the house my mom almost had a heart attack, 'cause
20   Muddy was standing there waggin' his tail, but Lee wasn't
21   anywhere to be found. I have to admit I was in a bit of a
22   panic, too, 'cause, even though he dissed my play, he's like,
23   still my brother, you know. So Mom's looking everywhere,
24   Dad's looking everywhere, and I'm looking everywhere. And
25   finally I found him. Under my bed, asleep. Poor little guy. I
26   don't think he's ever gonna want to stay home alone again.
27   Even if it means watching me in the school play.

39. Caroline's Birthday

1   Caroline broke up with me on Thursday. I was totally fine
2 by Friday. I was better than fine on Saturday. But on
3 Sunday, things all slid downhill. You see Sunday was
4 Caroline's birthday. Last year on Caroline's birthday we went
5 to "Movie Night Under the Stars" at Anderson Park. It was
6 super romantic. I even brought a picnic of sparkling cider,
7 crackers, and cheese. With a tiny little birthday cupcake and
8 one pink candle. Caroline was so happy. I was so happy. We
9 promised we'd love each other forever. Then about a year
10 passes and Thursday night Caroline tells me she just can't
11 see me anymore. She said it wasn't me, it was her. I said,
12 "Is there somebody else?" She swore up and down that
13 there wasn't. She said she just wanted to focus more on
14 school. She went into this big long story about how next
15 year she'll be applying to colleges and all that and how her
16 parents didn't want her to date for a while. I said, "Do you
17 still love me?" She said, "Oh, please, don't make this hard
18 for me, Brian. You know I do, but I just … can't anymore."
19 I swear I hate to admit it but I cried. But like I said, that was
20 Thursday. By Friday I was fine. And by Saturday I was even
21 better. But Sunday? Sunday on Caroline's birthday I had to
22 work. So I'm at Tony Bologna's Big Pie in the Sky waiting
23 on tables and doing my thing when in walks Caroline. With
24 a date! When I saw them I dropped a whole tray of cannolis.
25 Then it got worse. Tiny Tina, the hostess, starts taking
26 them over to my section. To my best booth. I went over to
27 Candy Peterson and I said, "Please Candy, please, please
28 take the party in booth number three. But Candy was deep

1   in the weeds. So, I considered my options. I decided there
2   were only a few things I could do. One: I could quit on the
3   spot and run out the back door. Two: I could purposely slide
4   on the dropped cannolis, break my head open, and be
5   carried out the door on a stretcher. Or Three: I could prove
6   to Caroline and Mr. Wonderful that I didn't care at all about
7   the break up. That I was already over her. So I went with
8   number three. And believe me it wasn't easy. Caroline and I
9   both just acted like we didn't know each other and it was
10 awkward as all get out. Especially when she went to the
11 restroom and this new guy called me over to tell me it was
12 "her birthday." I brought over the customary cannoli with a
13 candle and sang the special Tony Bologna birthday song.
14 Yeah, she got her cannoli alright. I'd like to say it wasn't one
15 of the ones I dropped on the floor. But hey, nobody's perfect,
16 right?

40. The Dating Game

1   Well, I guess that is what high school's all about, right?
2   The "Dating Game." Everybody's finding a date for Friday
3   night. Or everybody's finding a date for the prom. There's
4   always some excitement going on. And me? I haven't had
5   my first date yet, my first girlfriend, or my first kiss. Why?
6   Well, first of all my parents are very strict. There's no dating
7   in my family until you turn eighteen. That rule applies to all
8   of us. My sisters and me. So I'm almost seventeen. I'll be
9   seventeen next month as a matter of fact. That means, it
10   will be about another thirteen months and I'll be free to
11   date. That is, if I can get one. I'm just really shy around
12   girls. I don't know. It's funny, isn't it, because I've got five
13   sisters. On the other hand, maybe that's why I am shy.
14   Because I've got five sisters. Sometimes it gets to be too
15   much. My dad goes on a lot of business trips, so most of
16   the time, I'm the only guy. That gets a bit tiresome really.
17   About a year ago, I was telling my grandfather how I felt and
18   he offered to let me come and move into his garage. You
19   know, like a garage apartment. I really wanted to. I did. But,
20   I didn't have the nerve to ask my mom. It would've broken
21   her heart. It would have been fun though. So I didn't move
22   out and I'm still subjected to the girl world on a daily basis.
23   Sometimes I have to do the grocery shopping as part of my
24   weekly chores and that can be embarrassing, too. I hate it
25   when I have to buy, you know, feminine products. I had to
26   go through the checkout with them yesterday and the
27   manager couldn't ring me up and called for a price check.
28   How humiliating! Well, anyway, in a little over a year, like I

1   said, I'll be able to participate in all the fun. "The Dating
2   Game." But by then for me high school will be over. Weird,
3   right? I know. Oh, well, I'm a pretty fast learner, so that
4   should help. I just wish there was a rule book or something.
5   So I could start cramming, you know.

41. A Star in the House

1   *(Yelling to the other room)* **Mom! Will you tell Teresa that**
2   **she has to do the dishes tonight? I have a dress rehearsal**
3   **tomorrow and I need to study my lines. Thank you, Mommy.**
4   *(Sticks his tongue out at Teresa.)* **See, now? I told you so.** *(Goes*
5   *back to studying his lines. Then yelling to the other room)* **Mom!**
6   **Will you tell Louisa to turn off the TV or put on her**
7   **headphones? My lines! Thank you, Mommy dear.** *(Gives*
8   *Louisa a sardonic grin and goes back to studying. Then yelling to*
9   *the other room)* **Mom! Will you tell Dad that I have to sit in**
10 **this chair when I'm studying because it's my thinking chair?**
11 **Thank you, Mommy dearest.** *(Shrugs his shoulders at his dad*
12 *and gives a sheepish grin. Goes back to studying. Then yelling to*
13 *the other room)* **Mom! Will you tell Bowser that he has to stop**
14 **barking? I can't concentrate and I'm right in the middle of**
15 **studying my biggest scene. Thank you, Mommy dearest**
16 **love.** *(Sighs and looks at the audience.)* **It's hard having a star**
17 **like me in the house, I know. It's such an adjustment. They**
18 **just need a little time. They'll learn.**

42. Crazy Talk

1   There are only ten school days left until summer
2 vacation! Yes! I cannot wait. I hope these days go by so fast
3 my head spins. But I know they won't. Whenever you want
4 time to fly it goes slow. And whenever you want time to go
5 by slowly it goes really fast. Not sure what's going on with
6 that, but there's probably some scientific explanation. Don't
7 you think? So anyway, only ten more school days. Ten! And
8 then I'll be off to Hawaii with the folks. Man, I love summer
9 vacation. Dad and me, we're gonna go surfing and
10 snorkeling and jet skiing. It's gonna be an awesome time.
11 Mom will probably go hang out with the girls. Yeah, it's
12 gonna be paradise alright. And then next year, I'll be a
13 senior. Big man on campus! Whoa! How did that happen,
14 right? How many times did they threaten to hold me back a
15 year, right? But no way, man. I made it to senior year with
16 the rest of you dudes. So what are you guys doing over the
17 summer break? Working? Working as in doing work? What?
18 What's up with that? Since when? Since your parents think
19 you need some responsibility? Hey, I don't like the way that
20 sounds. Don't let them go talking to my parents, alright?
21 Yeah, thanks, man. Keep them far, far away. That's
22 dangerous talk right there. That's the kind of talk that could
23 put the big kibosh on catching waves all summer long.
24 Right? Yeah, that's crazy talk. I'm sorry dudes. I mean, that
25 totally, radically sucks. Wow! So you're like going to be
26 making money though, right? That's cool. Yeah, that's
27 totally cool. 'Cause when I come back in the fall, I might
28 totally need to borrow some cash.

43. Hold That Elevator, Please

Hold that elevator, please. *(Runs up to the elevator and manages to make it in before the doors close. Once inside looks around.)* Oh, no, it's you. If I'd known I'd have waited for the next elevator. Yeah, that's right. Look, it's hot enough in these elevators, so if you don't mind, try not to say anything so that you don't add to the hot air. *(The elevator comes to a sudden jerky stop.)* Hey, what just happened? What's going on? Why isn't the elevator moving? Why aren't the doors opening? Don't tell me we're stuck in here. Oh my gosh. Oh — my — gosh. I'm stuck in an elevator. *(Looks at girl.)* With you! *(Starts screaming.)* Help! Help! I'm stuck in the elevator with a maniac! *(Looks at her.)* Why aren't you screaming? Why are you so calm? You're a hysteric, crazy, whining, always has to get what you want kind of girl. What's with the suddenly serene demeanor? You've changed? You've changed? I find that hard to believe and yet … you do seem different. You do seem kind of … strange. In a good way, I mean. *(Breathing deeply)* So, has this ever happened to you before? No, not being stuck in an elevator with me. Being stuck in an elevator period. Me neither. *(Slides down against the wall and sits on the floor.)* I guess we better get comfortable. *(Watches her slide down to the floor, too.)* You know, actually, I'm sorry that we ended things on such bad terms. You, too? Really? It was a crazy time, right? A lot of stressful things going on in both of our lives. Yeah. It was just too hard. But still, there's no excuse for some of the things I said and did. Yeah, that's true. There's no excuse for some of the things you said and did either. I never

1 thought I'd hear you say that though. Wow! You really have
2 changed, haven't you? How did you do it? What did you do?
3 Oh. You fell in love. *(Looks disappointed.)* I see. So what we
4 had ... Yeah, I thought it was love too, but yeah, you're right.
5 It was infatuation. Nothing like ... the real thing. *(The elevator*
6 *doors open.)* Oh, thank goodness. Finally we can get out of
7 here. *(Walking out and turning to go)* Well. Good-bye.

44. Hopper

1   *(Hears the director call action.)* **When I was a little boy we**
2   **lived in a trailer park with lots of kids to play with. So I**
3   **remember it with fond memories. Cut!** *(Looks over to the*
4   *director.)* **I'm sorry, but I just don't think he'd say "fond**
5   **memories," do you? No, right? Yeah, right? OK, how 'bout if**
6   **he says ... OK, OK. Yeah, so I'll just cut that line. OK. OK.**
7   **Yeah, I'm ready.** *(Gets in place and waits. Hears the director call*
8   *action.)* **When I was a little boy we lived in a trailer park with**
9   **lots of kids to play with. There was one particular little girl**
10 **that I remember more than anyone else. La Hoppa was her**
11 **name. But I just called her Hopper. Cut!** *(Looks over at the*
12 *director.)* **Don't you think I should have a close-up there? No?**
13 **Are you sure? OK. Sorry! Yeah, Daddy-O, won't happen**
14 **again. Just trying to make sure we get this thing right. OK.**
15 **OK.** *(Gets into place and waits. Hears the director call action.)* **La**
16 **Hoppa was her name, but I just called her Hopper. She was**
17 **a pretty little girl with pearl white teeth. Her mother didn't**
18 **let her eat candy, but instead she kept a pocket full of dried**
19 **fish. Cut!** *(Looks at the director.)* **I'm sorry, but I don't know**
20 **why he says that? I mean, what's my motivation for that**
21 **line? A paycheck? Right? Got it. OK. OK. Sorry, folks.**
22 **Sorry, everyone. Right.** *(Gets into place and waits. Hears the*
23 *director call action.)* **Her mother didn't let her eat candy, but**
24 **instead she kept a pocket full of dried fish. Which I always**
25 **thought was strange. But now that I'm grown up, I don't**
26 **think it was strange at all. I think it was wonderful. And I**
27 **miss Hopper. I really do. I think of her often. Every time I**
28 **get a cavity. From all that candy I guess. Cut!** *(Looks at the*

1   *director again.)* **I'm sorry, but this scene totally doesn't make**

2   **sense. You agree? You do! Cool! So we'll rewrite the scene,**

3   **right?** *(Looks a bit worried.)* **We'll cut the scene? We'll cut the**

4   **character? You mean La Hoppa, right? Ah, I see. Well. I**

5   **know when I'm not wanted. I'll just be ... hopping along.**

45. Home Away from Home

1   I spend a lot of time at Ronnie's house. We work in his
2 garage with his dad. It's cool because they have a lot of
3 tools and stuff. We work on cars. We build things. And
4 Ronnie's dad treats me alright, you know. Almost better
5 than my own dad. Well, not really almost. Better. For sure.
6 It's not my dad's fault. He's just tired. He works really hard
7 in an office and doesn't get much time to spend at home.
8 When he is there he likes to watch TV. He doesn't talk a lot.
9 To me or to Mom. I feel more sorry for her than I do for
10 myself. At least I have Ronnie's house to escape to. Where
11 can she go? Nowhere, I guess. Yeah, I spend a lot of time at
12 Ronnie's. I eat dinner a lot there, too. His mom is really nice
13 and she cooks great. Don't get me wrong, my mom cooks
14 great, too. It's just different at Ronnie's. It's like dinner is
15 this fun event. Everyone gathers around the table and they
16 talk about their day and tell jokes. It seems like somebody's
17 always got some good news. At my house it's just the
18 opposite. Whenever my mom and dad have something to
19 say, it's usually not good news. *(Sighs.)* Oh, well. I sound
20 like a whiner, I guess. Yeah, I do. I mean, who am I to
21 complain? Lots of kids out there don't even have a mom and
22 dad. Or a place to sleep at night. Or food. Yeah, it's all
23 relative. So when you look at it that way, I've got it made.
24 I've not only got a home, but I've got Ronnie's house to go
25 to, too. A home away from home. Yeah, it's true. I've got it
26 made in the shade.

46. Doggone Dilemma

1   There's this little dog that lives in the apartment above
2 us who yaps nonstop. I sometimes wonder if he's a dog or
3 a barking machine. Like some kind of robot. He just barks
4 and barks and barks and barks and ... well, you get the
5 point. It's annoying. To say the least. We've tried
6 complaining to the leasing office, but they just seem to be
7 dumbfounded about what to do. They're like, "Gee whiz, we
8 told the owners and they're really sorry. The dog is probably
9 just getting used to it here." Getting used to it here? For six
10 months! I don't think so. That dog is a barking maniac. And
11 that is maniac spelled with a capital M. *Maniac! (Yells up at*
12 *the ceiling.) Did you hear me, Dog? Eh? You're not a dog,*
13 *you're a maniac.* Mom thinks I'm starting to lose it, but
14 that's nonsense. You can see that I'm being really rational,
15 right? I'm just asserting my right to be heard. The dog gets
16 to be heard, right? No matter what time of day or night. The
17 dog can talk all he wants. Huh? Yeah, of course a dog can't
18 talk. I said bark. No, I didn't say talk. I said the dog can
19 bark all he wants. *(Imitates the dog.)* Yip. Yip. Yap. Yap. Yap.
20 Yip. Roof, roof, roof. I can be doing my homework and still I
21 hear Yip, Yip, Yap. Yap. Yap. Yip. Roof, roof, woooof. I could
22 be trying to sleep and still I hear ... well, you get the picture.
23 Any ideas? Please, I need some help here. I mean, I'm not
24 on the verge of a nervous breakdown or anything. I'm just
25 ... dog-tired.

47. Leaving Home?

1   Tomorrow I'm leaving. For good. I've packed my things
2 and I'm ready to go. Set my alarm for the crack of dawn.
3 Gonna get up before everyone else and leave nothing behind
4 but this here note. Yeah, the folks are gonna be in for a
5 surprise. Kids, too. They'll find out they won't be able to
6 push me around anymore and then what will they do? Who
7 will they yell at and curse and treat like dirt when I'm gone?
8 *(Pauses and thinks for a moment.)* I don't know why they
9 always treated me different. But they did. There wasn't
10 anything I did to deserve it. Far as I could see. They just
11 always have treated me like I'm different from the rest. Like
12 I'm a boarder in this house. Like I don't deserve one morsel
13 they've put in my mouth. *(Takes a deep breath.)* But I don't
14 know why I'm going on and on about it. Tomorrow it's all
15 gonna come to an end. Yes, sir. I'm leaving ... this place.
16 You know I almost said "home." Yep, I almost said, "I'm
17 leaving home." I could never say that with an honest heart.
18 This place just ain't never been a home to me.

48. Painting Fences

1   *(Facing the audience and miming that he's painting a big*
2   *green picket fence)* **Howdy, folks. Nice of you to join me. My**
3   **name is Ben and I'm just painting this fence. It's a nice**
4   **green color don't you think? Kind of green like the grass**
5   **under my feet. Not sure what ya'll are doing here, but it's**
6   **mighty nice of you to want to watch. Feels like this job**
7   **won't be so lonely now. Yeah, sure, painting can be a lonely**
8   **proposition. Well,** *(Looks down the line of the fence.)* **you take**
9   **this fence for instance. This fence stretches down well over**
10   **a mile. That's a lot of painting and I don't have a helper. So**
11   **that's a long time I'm out here by myself. With no one to talk**
12   **to. Except, well, now I'm talking to you. So you see, I'm**
13   **mighty glad to see you here. It's a beautiful day, too.** *(Looks*
14   *up.)* **Just look at that sky. If I were a different kind of**
15   **painter, you know, like an artistic type, I'd like to paint that**
16   **sky. Wouldn't you? I'm always thinking that though.**
17   **Standing in some field painting some fence, one color, one**
18   **same old color, up and down, up and down, and dreaming**
19   **about painting the sky, or a bird, or some rabbit hopping**
20   **across the grass. Yes, sir. Even a guy who paints fences can**
21   **have a dream.**

49. The Call That Changed My Life

1   I've spent the last three years in Southern California for
2   pilot season. My mom and I came out when she realized that
3   this little dream of mine, to be a star, was not gonna go away.
4   Yes, that's right, a star. Acting in the school play or the local
5   community theater was not enough for me. I wanted to make
6   m-o-n-e-y. That's right. The green stuff. And plenty of it. So
7   Mom and Dad agreed that she'd come out with me and Dad
8   would support us from back home. And we never looked back.
9   I've done a gazillion auditions and classes, too. Had a lot of
10   callbacks. Which they say is a huge accomplishment. It never
11   feels like it though. Unless you get the part, I guess. I wouldn't
12   know. 'Cause, three years or not. It hasn't happened for me
13   yet. Yeah, sad but true. It's not uncommon though, so I
14   shouldn't feel like a failure. I know that I shouldn't, but I
15   sometimes do. Yeah, it's hard. The other day I went on this
16   audition that felt just right. I mean, it felt like I was just right
17   for the part. Then I got a callback and that felt just right, too.
18   In fact, the casting director said I did an amazing job. I just
19   knew that this was going to be my lucky break. Mom and I
20   were so excited and so nervous. We knew that we would know
21   if I'd been cast by the end of the day. So we waited for the call.
22   And sure enough, around 5:00 PM Mom's cell phone rang, but
23   it was Grandma. Dad had a heart attack and is in the ICU.
24   Mom flew back right away and I'm going back tomorrow. I had
25   an audition today, so I stayed behind with the Burkes. I mean,
26   it sounds really cold, but this could be the big one, right? And
27   to be honest, once I get on that plane tomorrow, I don't think
28   I'll be coming back. Yep, I finally got it. The call that changed
29   my life.

50. Good-bye

1   Taylor and I are meeting tonight. One last time. *(Sighs.)*
2 Yes, that inevitable moment has arrived. The time to say
3 good-bye. I always knew this day would come, but now that
4 it's here, I don't know if I can face it. I'm gonna miss Taylor
5 so much. We're like, soulmates. And the times we've had
6 have been ... the best. So saying good-bye is the last thing
7 I want to do. But I have to. Right? I'm at the mercy of life.
8 And life is so weird sometimes. Everything is so ...
9 temporary. Me and Taylor. This past year. It all just flew by
10 like the blink of an eye. *(Pauses to think.)* It would be easy
11 just to blame Mom. I mean, when she took this job five
12 years ago she knew that we'd have to move every twelve
13 months. She knew what that would mean for me. Always
14 changing schools. Always having to make new friends. And
15 always having to say good-bye. And believe me, I haven't
16 been shy about expressing myself with Mom. She's heard all
17 the complaints. She knows how I feel. And she always says,
18 "Life would change whether we move or not." She says,
19 "Even if we stayed in the same place forever, nothing would
20 stay the same. People change. People leave. People die."
21 *(Pauses to think about that for a moment.)* **She's right. I mean,**
22 even if we never left Louisville things wouldn't be the same.
23 Already, when Dad died, everything changed. Then Mom
24 took this job and ever since then we've been constantly on
25 the go. We've lived in Florida, Texas, Alabama, and
26 Tennessee, just in the past five years alone. And tomorrow
27 we're off to Washington State. I asked Mom the other night
28 if she thought we might one day just settle in one place

1   again. For good. She said, "Probably not. But I never say
2   never." I'm not sure what that meant, but it gave me a little
3   hope. A tiny speck of hope, anyway. For the future. But for
4   now? I've got to go meet Taylor and say the word I've come
5   to hate. "Good-bye."

About the Author

Mary holds a B.A. in Acting/Directing from Florida Atlantic University where she studied with Edward Albee and Joshua Logan. She also studied opera and performed in *The Medium* by Carlo Menotti and *La Serva Padrona* by Giovanni Battista Pergolesi.

Mary Depner taught drama for ten years and has directed and performed in countless plays.

Mary's published writings include *Sugared and Spiced: 100 Monologues for Girls*, *Echo Booming Monologues: 100 Monologues for Teens*, and *Smart Monologues: Vocabulary Building Monologues for Teens and Adults* published by Jelliroll, Inc. and *50/50 Monologues for Student Actors* (Meriwether Publishing Ltd.). Mary is delighted to be published with Meriwether Publishing and looks forward to writing many more books in the future.

In addition to writing for the stage, Mary enjoys singing, reading, and watching independent and foreign films.

Order Form

Meriwether Publishing Ltd.
PO Box 7710
Colorado Springs, CO 80933-7710
Phone: 800-937-5297   Fax: 719-594-9916
Website: www.meriwether.com

Please send me the following books:

_____ **50/50 Monologues for Student Actors II**   **$16.95**
#BK-B330
by Mary Depner
100 more monologues for guys and girls

_____ **50/50 Monologues for Student Actors**   **$15.95**
#BK-B321
by Mary Depner
100 monologues for guys and girls

_____ **102 Great Monologues #BK-B315**   **$16.95**
by Rebecca Young
A versatile collection of monologues and duologues for student actors

_____ **Famous Fantasy Character Monologs**   **$16.95**
#BK-B286
by Rebecca Young
Starring the Not-So-Wicked Witch and more

_____ **100 Great Monologs #BK-B276**   **$15.95**
by Rebecca Young
A collection of monologs, duologs and triologs for actors

_____ **Winning Monologs for Young Actors**   **$15.95**
#BK-B127
by Peg Kehret
Honest-to-life monologs for young actors

_____ **Improv Ideas #BK-B283**   **$24.95**
by Justine Jones and Mary Ann Kelley
A book of games and lists

These and other fine Meriwether Publishing books are available at your local bookstore or direct from the publisher. Prices subject to change without notice. Check our website or call for current prices.

Name: _____ email:_____

Organization name: _____

Address: _____

City: _____ State: _____

Zip: _____ Phone: _____

❑ **Check enclosed**

❑ **Visa / MasterCard / Discover / Am. Express #** _____

| | Expiration | CVV |
Signature: _____ date: _____ / _____ code: _____
   (required for credit card orders)

Colorado residents: Please add 3% sales tax.
Shipping: Include $3.95 for the first book and 75¢ for each additional book ordered.

❑ *Please send me a copy of your complete catalog of books and plays.*

Order Form

Meriwether Publishing Ltd.
PO Box 7710
Colorado Springs, CO 80933-7710
Phone: 800-937-5297   Fax: 719-594-9916
Website: www.meriwether.com

Please send me the following books:

_____ **50/50 Monologues for Student Actors II**   **$16.95**
#BK-B330
by Mary Depner
100 more monologues for guys and girls

_____ **50/50 Monologues for Student Actors**   **$15.95**
#BK-B321
by Mary Depner
100 monologues for guys and girls

_____ **102 Great Monologues #BK-B315**   **$16.95**
by Rebecca Young
A versatile collection of monologues and duologues for student actors

_____ **Famous Fantasy Character Monologs**   **$16.95**
#BK-B286
by Rebecca Young
Starring the Not-So-Wicked Witch and more

_____ **100 Great Monologs #BK-B276**   **$15.95**
by Rebecca Young
A collection of monologs, duologs and triologs for actors

_____ **Winning Monologs for Young Actors**   **$15.95**
#BK-B127
by Peg Kehret
Honest-to-life monologs for young actors

_____ **Improv Ideas #BK-B283**   **$24.95**
by Justine Jones and Mary Ann Kelley
A book of games and lists

These and other fine Meriwether Publishing books are available at your local bookstore or direct from the publisher. Prices subject to change without notice. Check our website or call for current prices.

Name: _____ email:_____

Organization name: _____

Address: _____

City: _____ State: _____

Zip: _____ Phone: _____

❑ **Check enclosed**

❑ **Visa / MasterCard / Discover / Am. Express #** _____

Signature: _____   Expiration date: _____ / _____   CVV code: _____
        (required for credit card orders)

Colorado residents: Please add 3% sales tax.
Shipping: Include $3.95 for the first book and 75¢ for each additional book ordered.

❑ *Please send me a copy of your complete catalog of books and plays.*